T0114826

Summer
Kakuro

Pete Sinden is an expert in the creation of Intelligent Systems. His computer software is used in more than a hundred American universities. Applying artificial intelligence, game theory, computer modelling and simulation techniques, he creates puzzles for pleasure. He has degrees from the University of Oxford, University College London and the University of Georgia, USA. He also holds directorships for several companies and is the author of many internationally bestselling Su Doku titles.

Summer
Kakuro

PETE SINDEN

ATRIA BOOKS

New York   London   Toronto   Sydney

ATRIA BOOKS
A Division of Simon & Schuster, Inc.
1230 Avenue of the Americas
New York, NY 10020

First Atria Books trade paperback edition July 2007

ATRIA BOOKS and colophon are trademarks
of Simon & Schuster, Inc.

For information about special discounts for bulk
purchases, please contact Simon & Schuster Special Sales
at 1-800-456-6798 or business@simonandschuster.com.

Manufactured in the United States of America

1   3   5   7   9   10   8   6   4   2

ISBN-13: 978-0-7432-9750-9
ISBN-10:   0-7432-9750-4

Contents

Introduction

Puzzles

Solutions

Cheat Sheets

Summer **Kakuro**

Introduction

What is Kakuro?

Kakuro is an extremely addictive puzzle game—a test of skill and logic. All you have to do is place numbers 1 to 9 on the puzzle grid. Easy!

Or is it? Only one arrangement of numbers will give the correct answer. It can be seductively simple or it can be mind-bending. This book contains 201 Kakuro puzzles at four levels of difficulty (Piece of Cake, Tea Break, Lunch Break and All Nighter)—enough to satisfy beginners and addicts alike for hours on end.

How to play Kakuro

The diagram overleaf shows a small Kakuro puzzle. The objective is to place numbers 1 to 9 in the white cells on the grid, so that each row or column of adjoining white cells adds up to the total printed in the dark grey cell to their left (for a row) or above (for a column). The light grey cells do not play any part in the game.

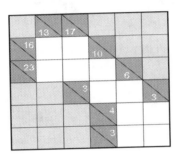

YOU MUST place the numbers 1 to 9 in the white cells in the unique arrangement so that all the column and row totals are correct.

YOU MUST NOT repeat a number in any continuous row or column of white cells.

How to crack Kakuro

Begin by looking at the totals (the dark grey cells)—these are your first clues.

For example:

Looking at the puzzle shown, and starting in its simplest area, the bottom row, there are two white cells that must add together to make 3 (the value marked in the dark grey cell to their left).

We know that 1 + 2 = 3. Any other combination of two numbers between 1 and 9, where no number is repeated, will add up to a value greater than 3, so this row must contain 1 and 2.

All we have to do now is determine the order in which they should appear: is it [1,2] or [2,1]? To do this we must look at the neighbouring cells.

Look first at the two cells in the row above. We are told these contain two numbers that add to make 4. 1 + 3 is the only combination of two numbers that add to make 4, without repeating a number (2 + 2 would repeat the value 2).

Look next at the far right column of the grid. It contains two numbers that add to make 3, so we know it must contain a 1 and a 2 (using the same reasoning that we used for the bottom row).

So which number goes in which cell?

Let's try a few combinations and see how we get on. First we will try placing the numbers 1 and 2 in the bottom row in the order [2,1].

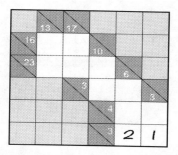

If we do this we must place a 2 in the last cell of the row above, to make the far right column add up to 3. However, as this cell's row must be made up of a 1 and a 3, to give a total of 4, placing a 2 must be wrong.

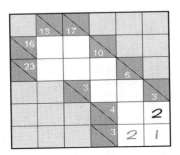

Therefore we must go back and try placing the numbers in the bottom row in a different order [1,2], and then follow the same logical steps to see if this results in a better outcome.

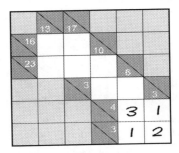

As we can see, all the numbers we have placed now add up to the correct column and row totals without repeating any value in any row or column. In fact, they also allow us to make the leap quickly to filling in a 2 in the only open white cell in the fourth column, to give the required column total of 6.

In larger puzzles, several continuous blocks of white cells may appear in a single row (as in a crossword). While you must not repeat a value in any adjoining white cells, you may repeat values across the whole row or column providing they fall in separate groups of white cells. The example below should explain this clearly:

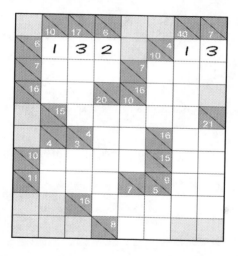

As can be seen, the numbers 1 and 3 appear twice in the top row. This is perfectly correct as they do not appear more than once in either of the two continuous blocks of adjoining white cells.

Conclusion

When you first see a Kakuro puzzle, you may think it is all about maths. Don't be fooled. And don't panic. It isn't. Only simple sums are ever used and these are repeated time and again, so quickly become second nature.

But for anyone who wasn't paying attention (or prefers never to add), cheat sheets are included at the back of this book listing by total all the possible valid number combinations from 1 to 9.

Arranging the numbers is the challenge!

Then starts the addiction . . .

Kakuro will drive you crazy.

The greatest challenge will be putting it down . . .

Summer **Kakuro**

Piece of Cake

Puzzles 1–40

Puzzle 1

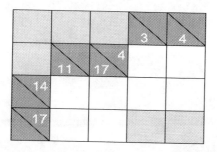

Puzzle 2

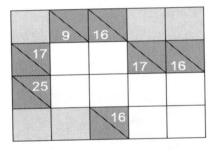

Piece of Cake

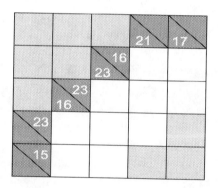

Puzzle 4

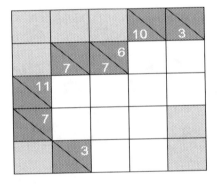

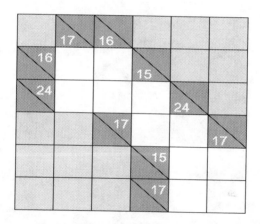

Puzzle 6

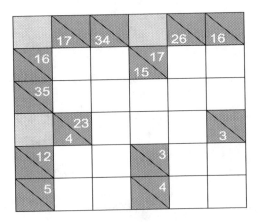

Piece of Cake

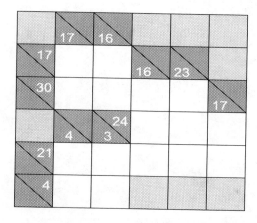

Puzzle 8

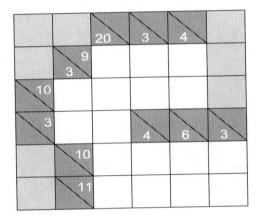

Piece of Cake

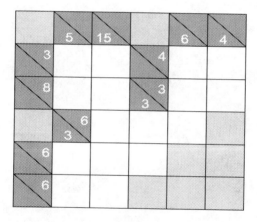

Puzzle 10

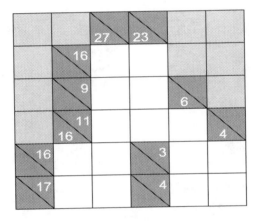

Piece of Cake

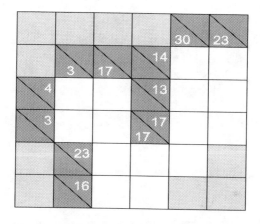

Puzzle 12

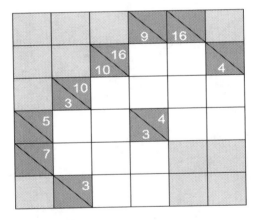

Piece of Cake

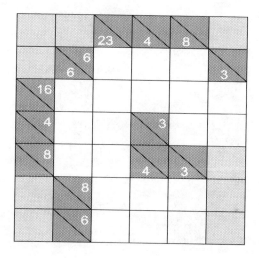

Puzzle 14

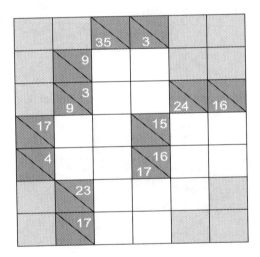

Piece of Cake

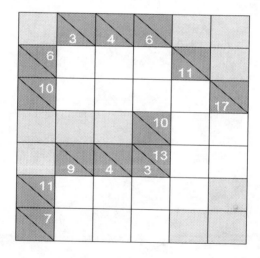

Puzzle 16

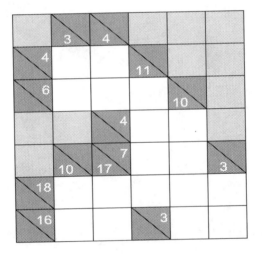

Piece of Cake

Puzzle 17

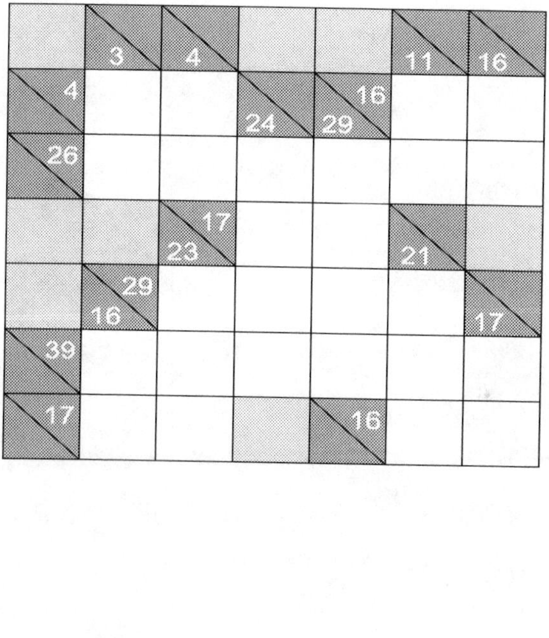

Puzzle 18

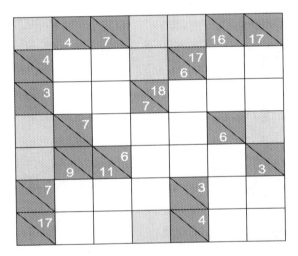

Piece of Cake

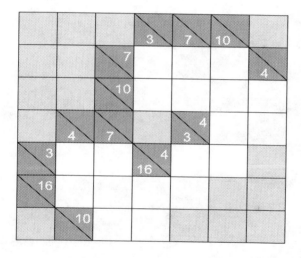

Puzzle 20

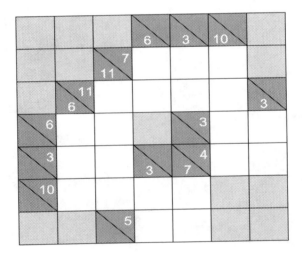

Piece of Cake

Puzzle 21

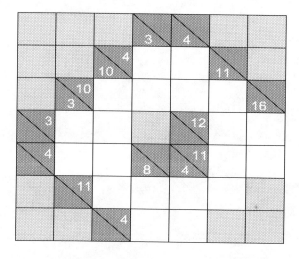

Puzzle 22

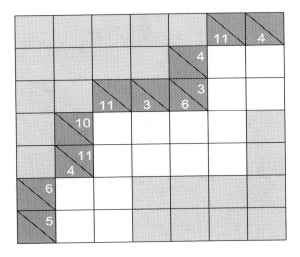

Piece of Cake

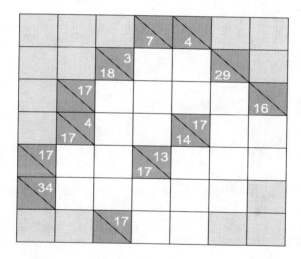

Puzzle 24

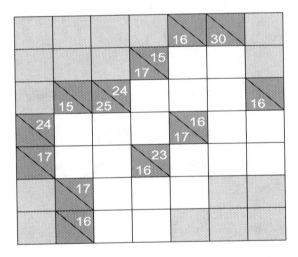

Piece of Cake

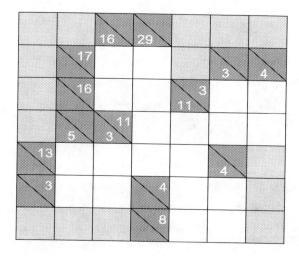

Puzzle 26

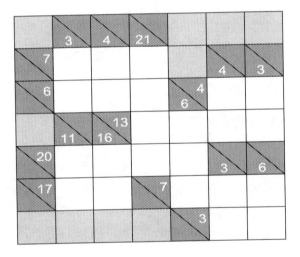

Piece of Cake

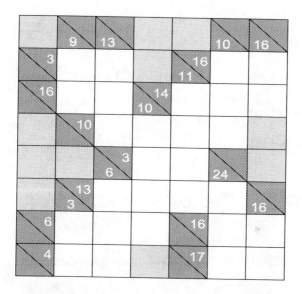

Puzzle 28

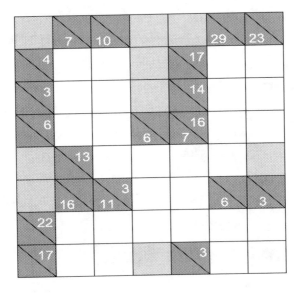

Piece of Cake

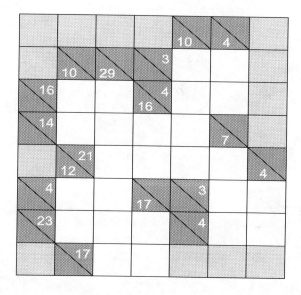

Puzzle 30

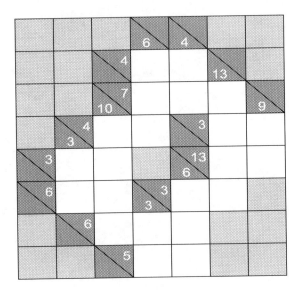

Piece of Cake

Puzzle 31

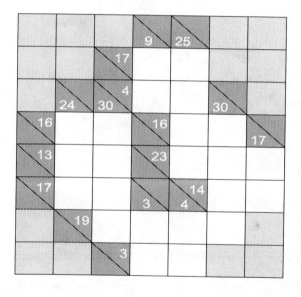

Puzzle 32

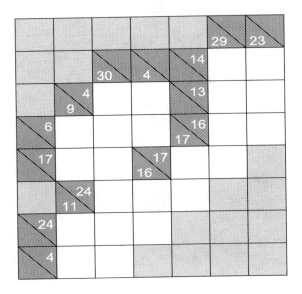

Piece of Cake

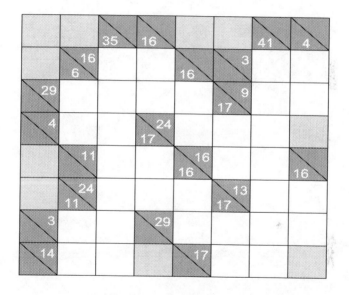

Puzzle 34

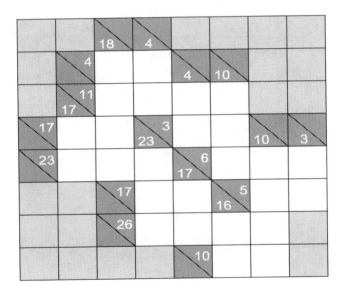

Piece of Cake

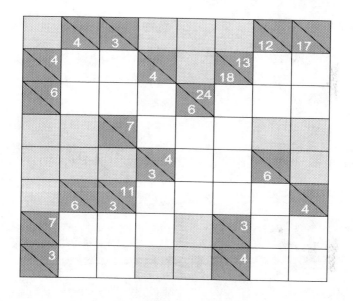

Puzzle 36

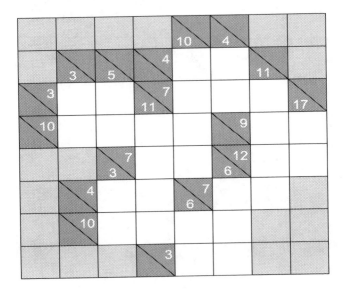

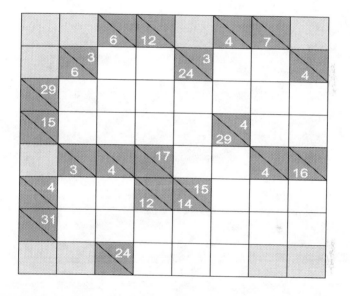

Puzzle 38

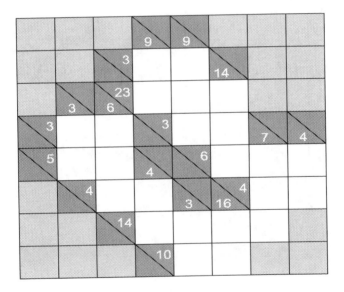

Piece of Cake

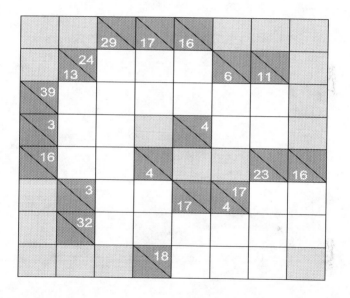

Puzzle 40

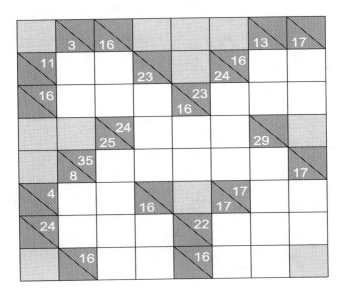

Piece of Cake

Summer **Kakuro**

Tea Break

Puzzles 41–110

Puzzle 41

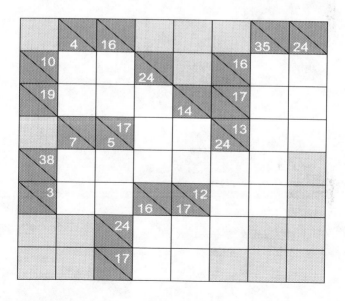

Puzzle 42

Tea Break

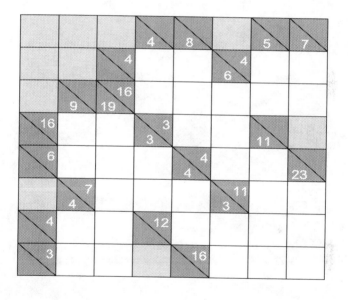

Puzzle 44

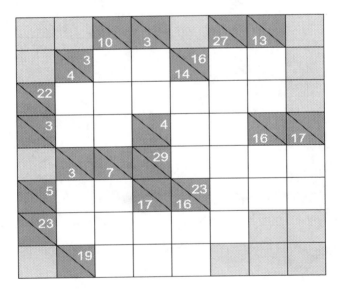

Tea Break

Puzzle 45

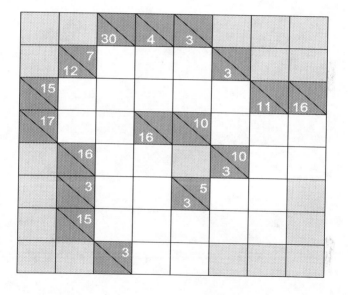

Puzzle 46

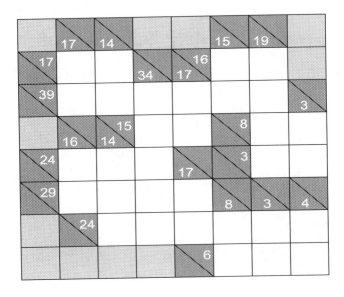

Tea Break

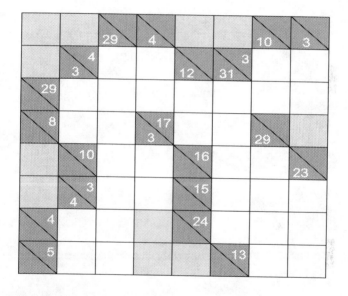

Puzzle 48

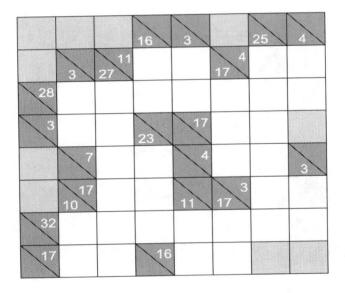

Tea Break

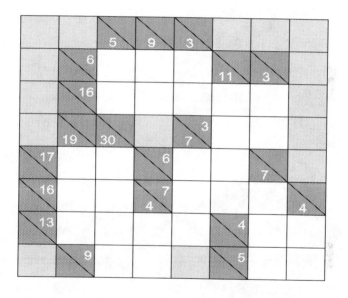

Puzzle 50

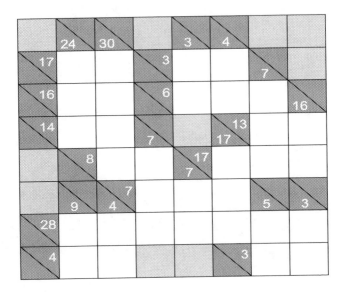

Tea Break

Puzzle 51

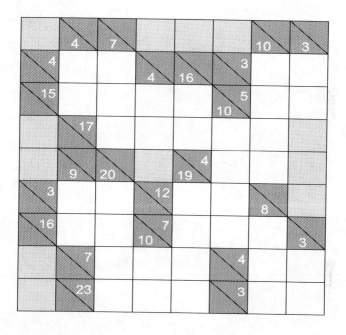

Puzzle 52

Tea Break

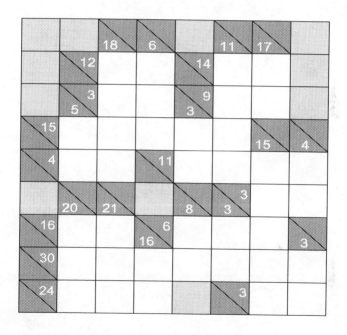

Puzzle 54

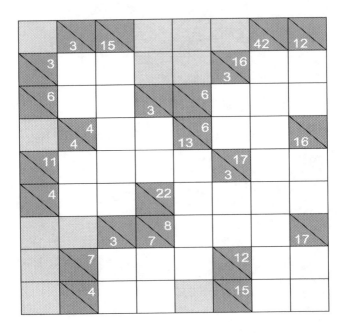

Tea Break

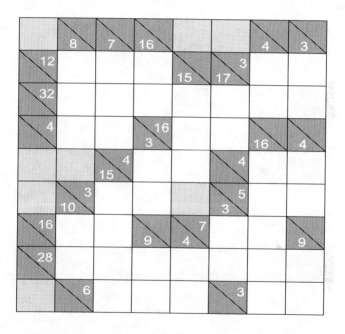

Puzzle 56

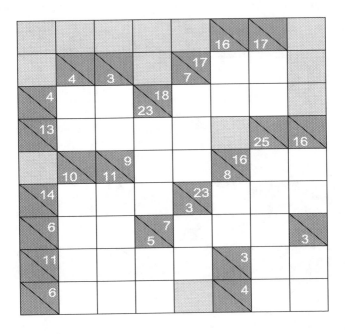

Tea Break

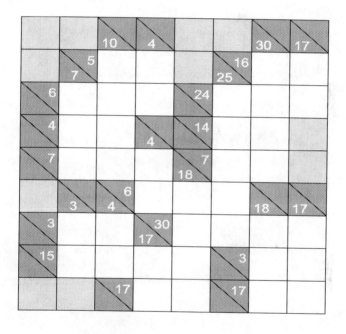

Puzzle 58

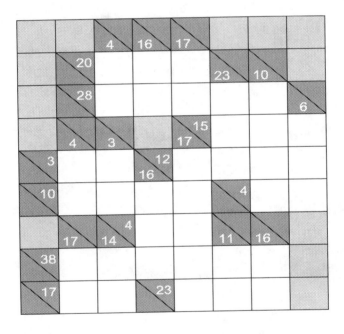

Tea Break

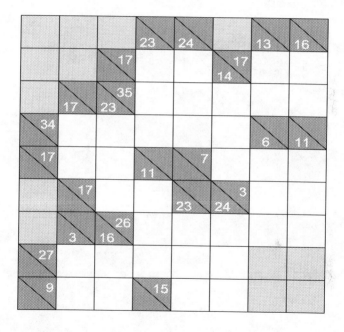

Puzzle 60

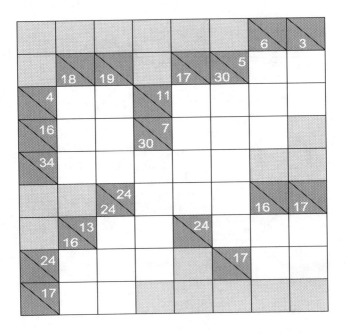

Tea Break

Puzzle 61

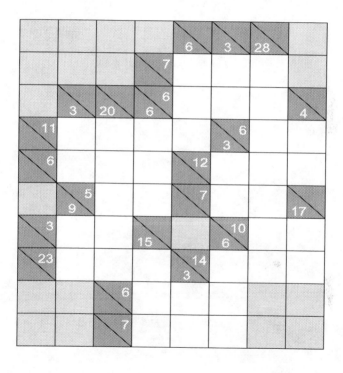

Puzzle 62

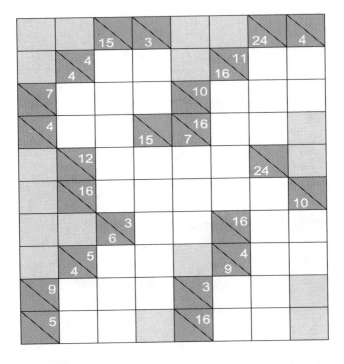

Tea Break

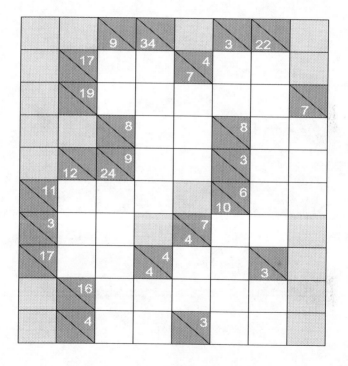

Puzzle 64

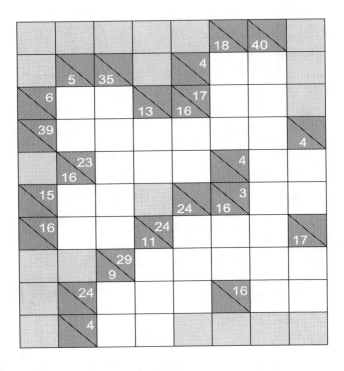

Tea Break

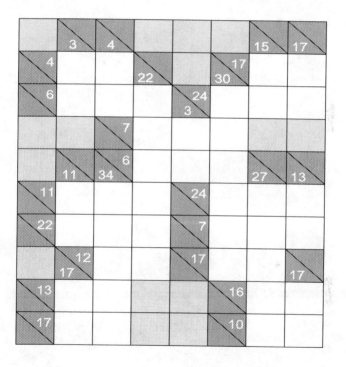

Puzzle 66

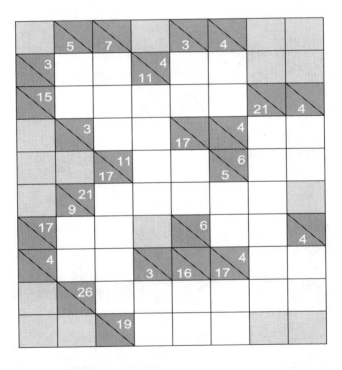

Tea Break

Puzzle 67

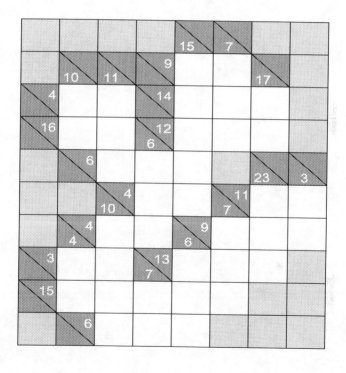

Puzzle 68

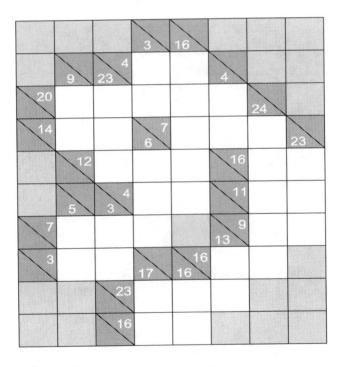

Tea Break

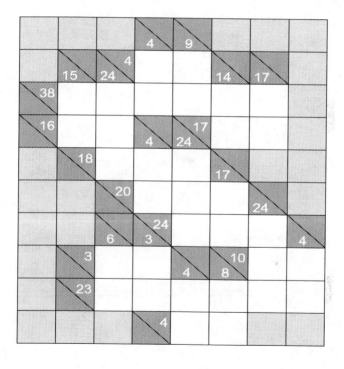

Puzzle 70

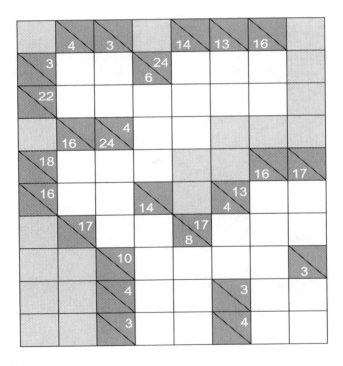

Tea Break

Puzzle 71

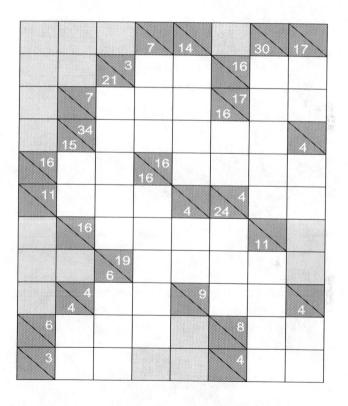

Puzzle 72

Tea Break

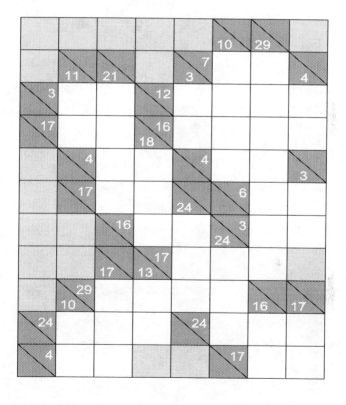

Puzzle 74

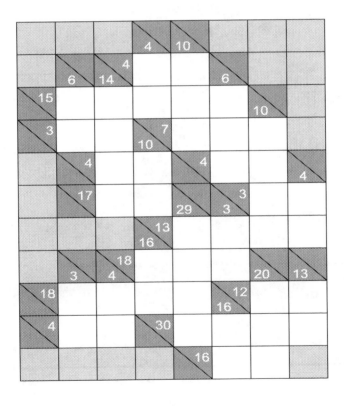

Tea Break

Puzzle 75

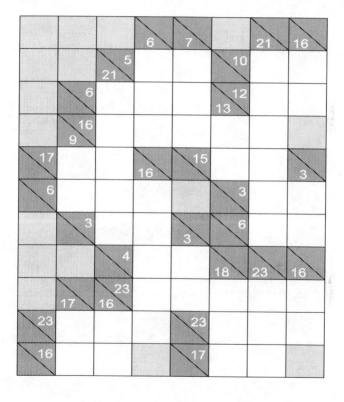

Puzzle 76

Tea Break

Puzzle 78

Tea Break

Puzzle 80

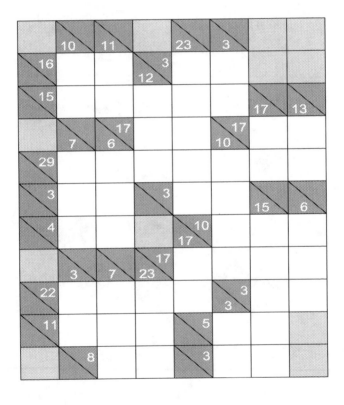

Tea Break

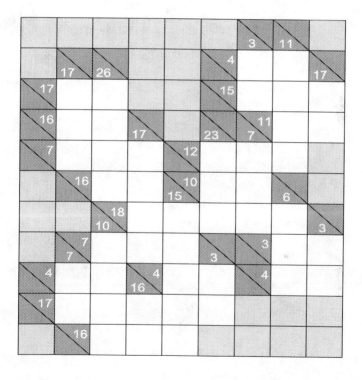

Puzzle 82

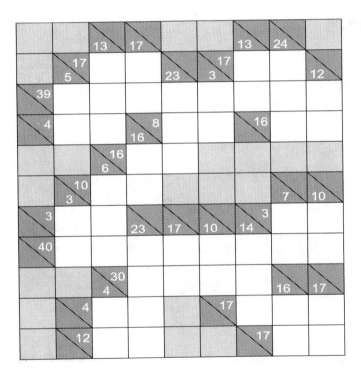

Tea Break

Puzzle 83

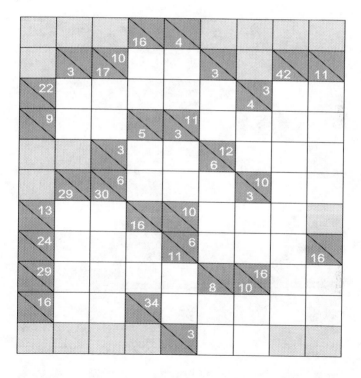

Puzzle 84

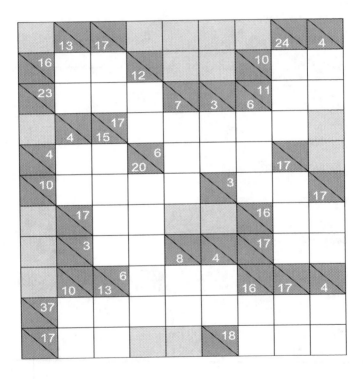

Tea Break

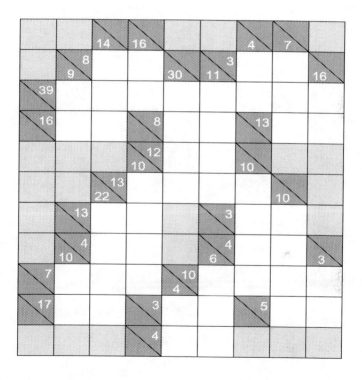

Puzzle 86

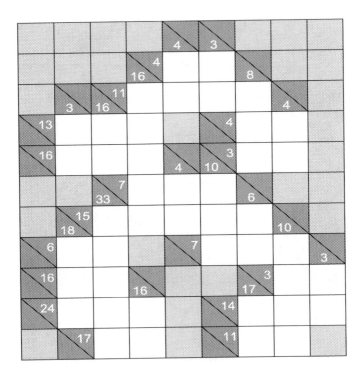

Tea Break

Puzzle 87

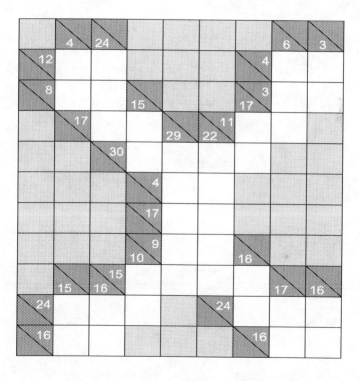

Puzzle 88

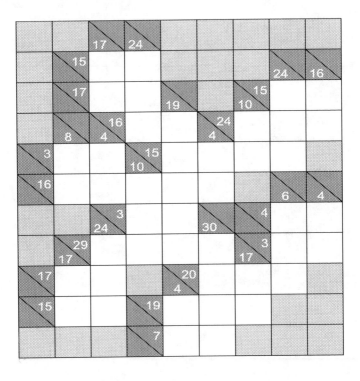

Tea Break

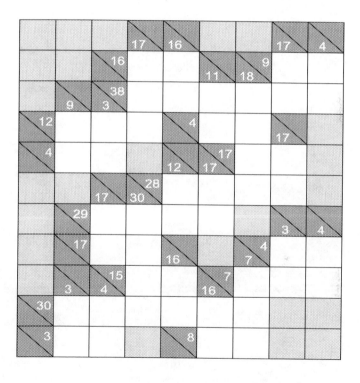

Puzzle 90

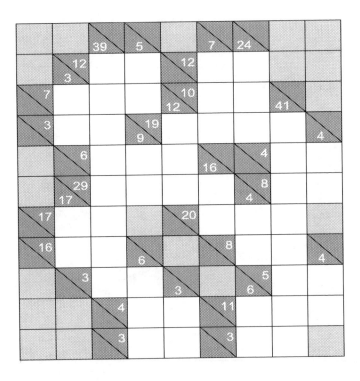

Tea Break

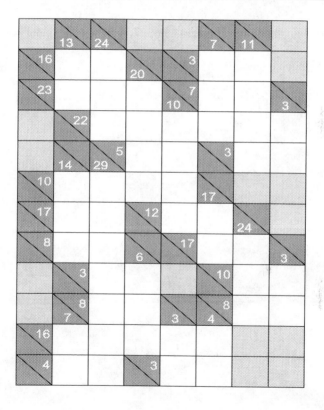

Puzzle 92

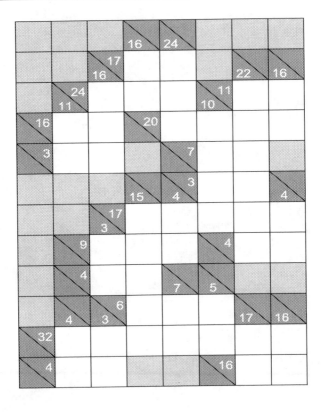

Tea Break

Puzzle 94

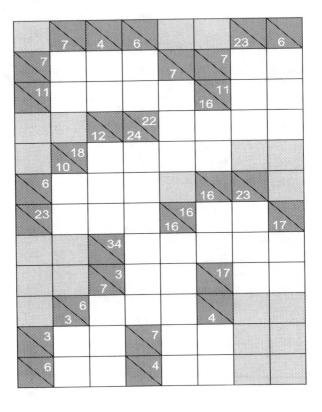

Tea Break

Puzzle 96

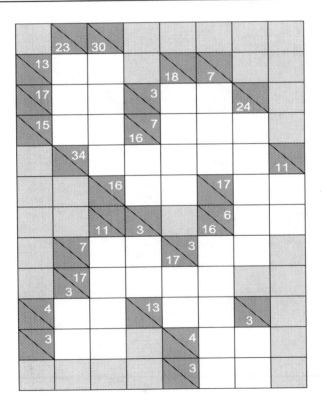

Tea Break

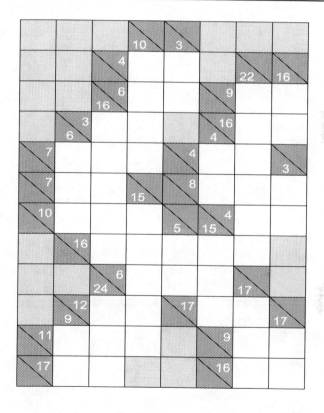

Puzzle 98

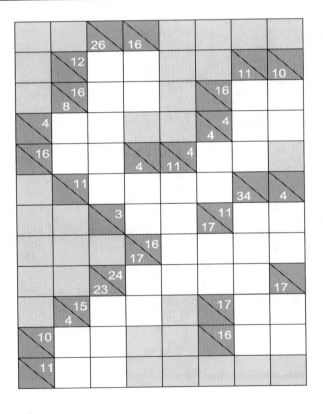

Tea Break

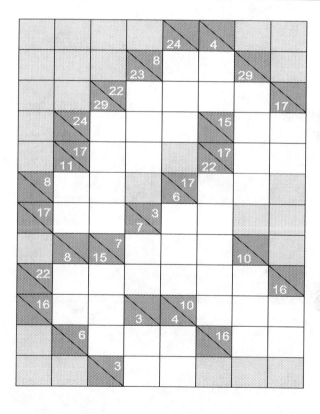

Puzzle 100

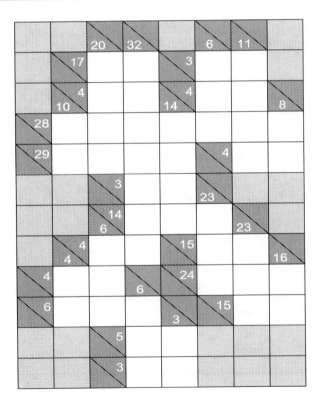

Tea Break

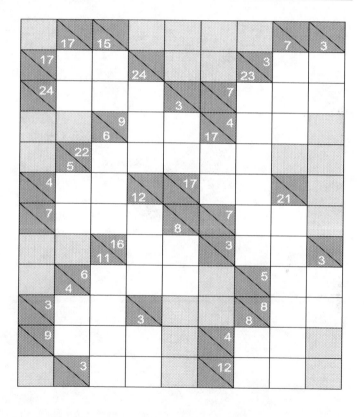

Puzzle 102

Tea Break

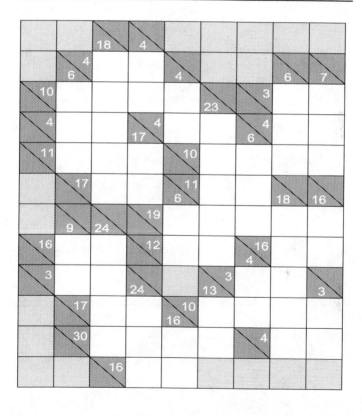

Puzzle 104

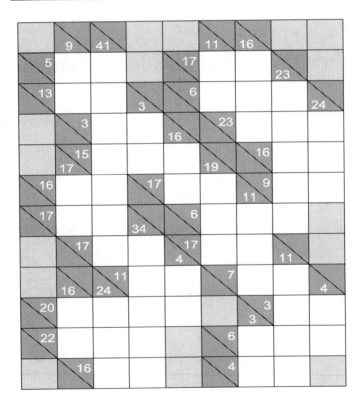

Tea Break

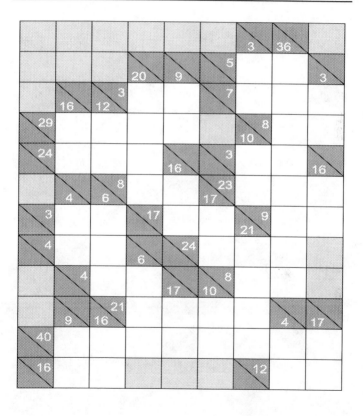

Puzzle 106

Tea Break

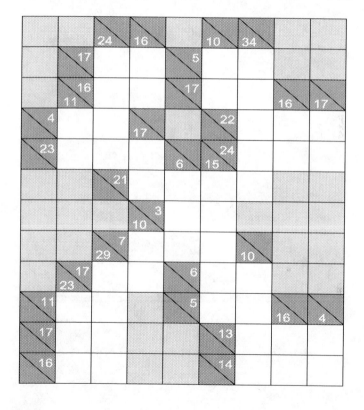

Puzzle 108

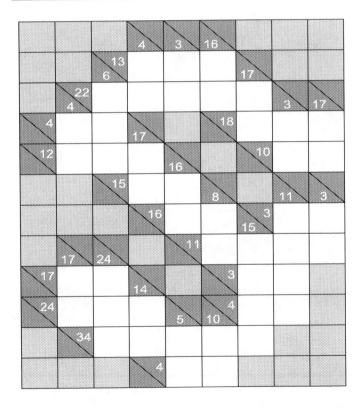

Tea Break

Puzzle 109

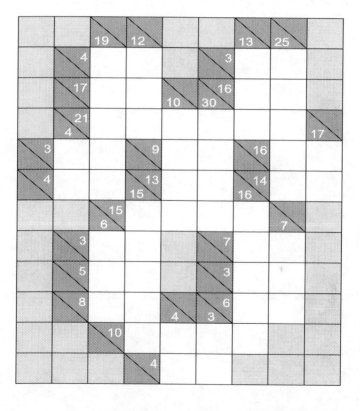

Puzzle 110

Tea Break

Summer **Kakuro**

Lunch Break

Puzzles 111–180

Puzzle 111

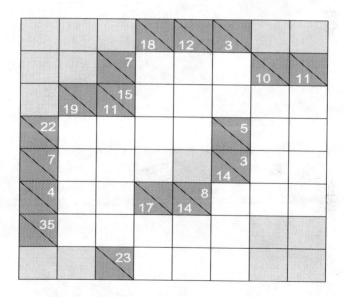

Puzzle 112

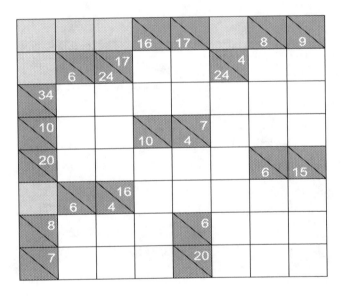

Lunch Break

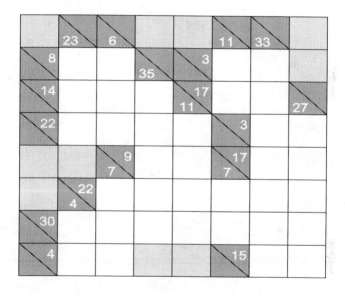

Puzzle 114

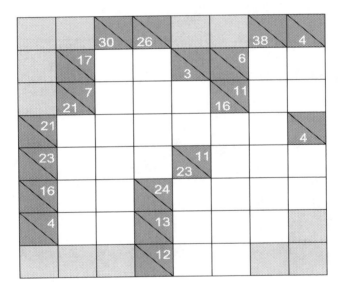

Lunch Break

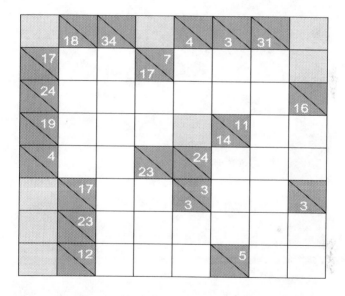

Puzzle 116

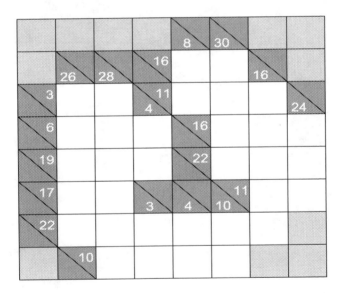

Lunch Break

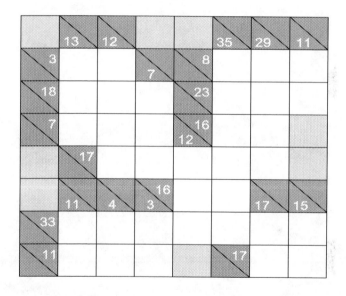

Puzzle 118

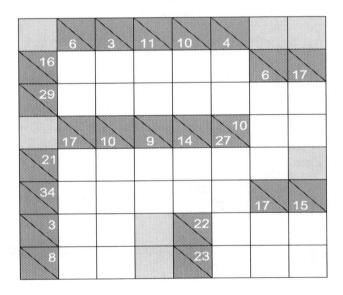

Lunch Break

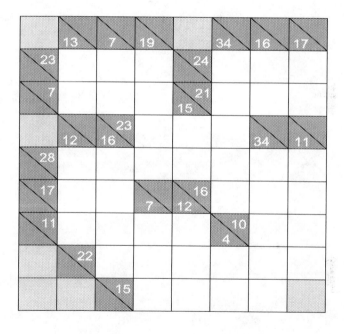

Puzzle 120

Lunch Break

Puzzle 121

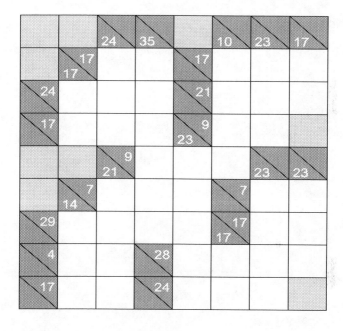

Puzzle 122

Lunch Break

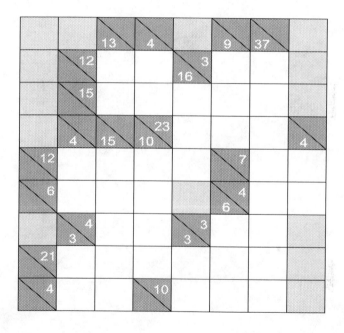

Puzzle 124

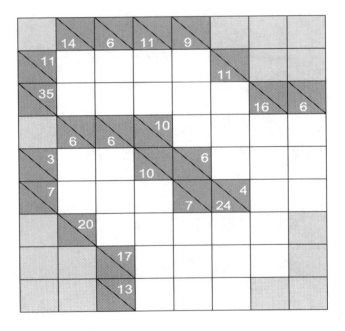

Lunch Break

Puzzle 125

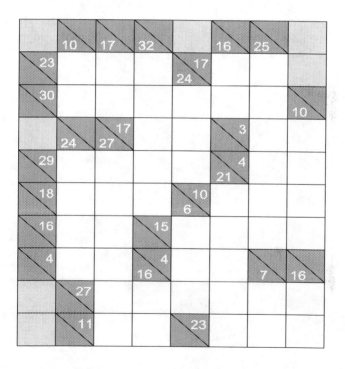

Puzzles 111–180

Puzzle 126

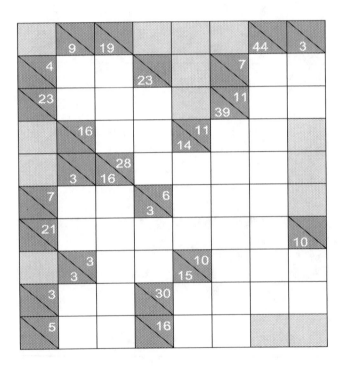

Lunch Break

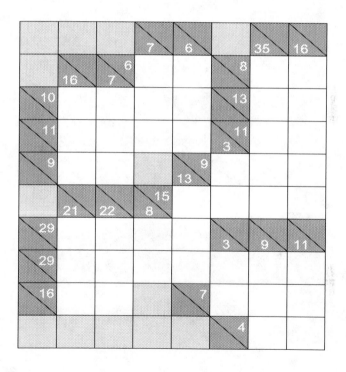

Puzzle 128

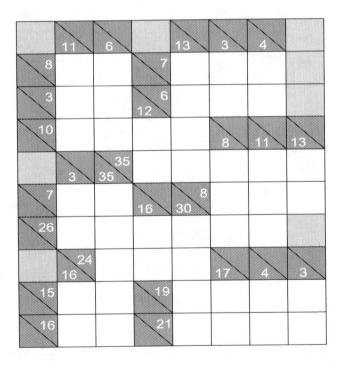

Lunch Break

Puzzle 129

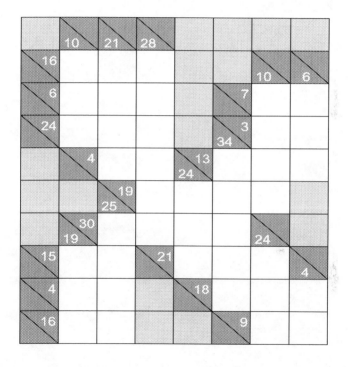

Puzzle 130

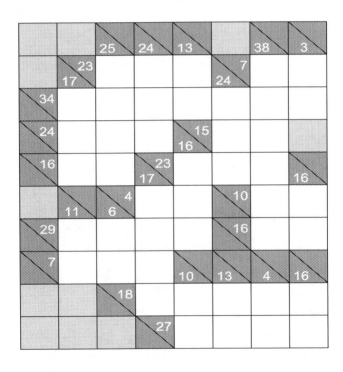

Lunch Break

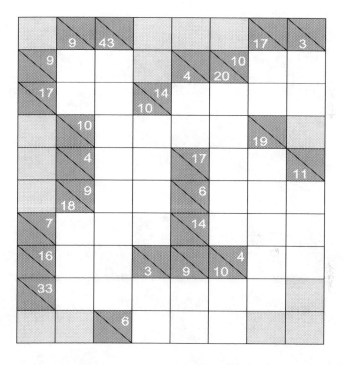

Puzzle 132

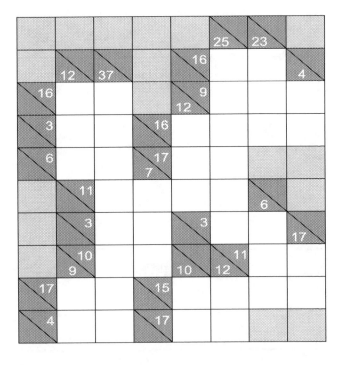

Lunch Break

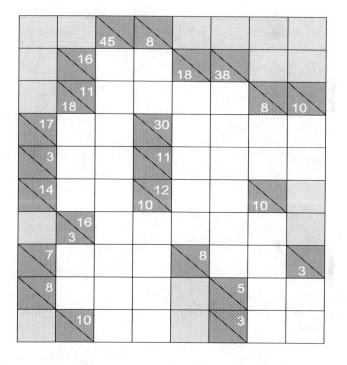

Puzzle 134

Lunch Break

Puzzle 135

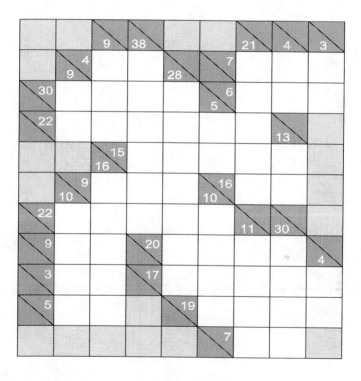

Puzzle 136

Lunch Break

Puzzle 137

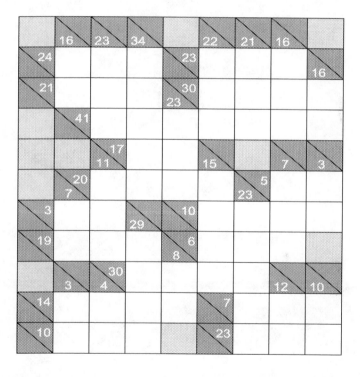

Puzzle 138

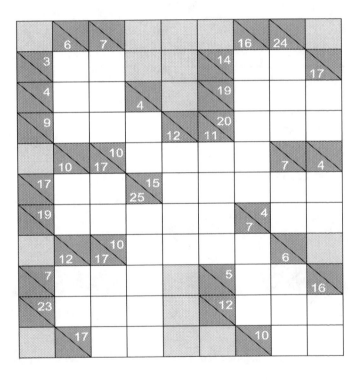

Lunch Break

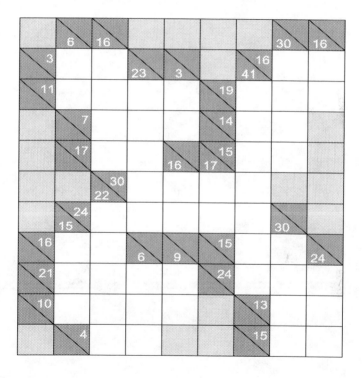

Puzzle 140

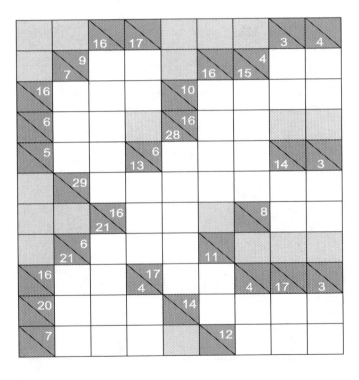

Lunch Break

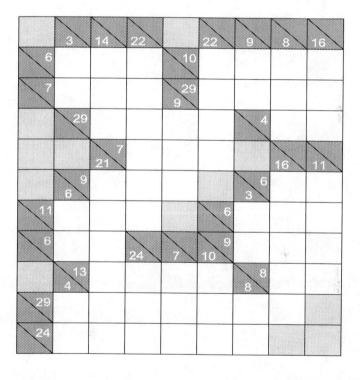

Puzzle 142

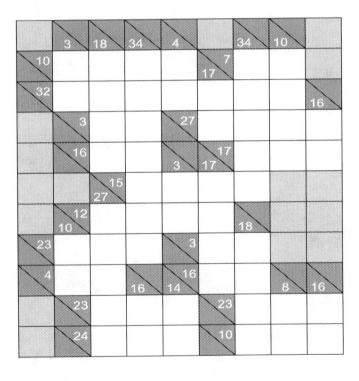

Lunch Break

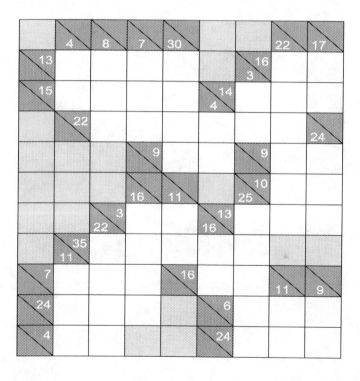

Puzzle 144

Lunch Break

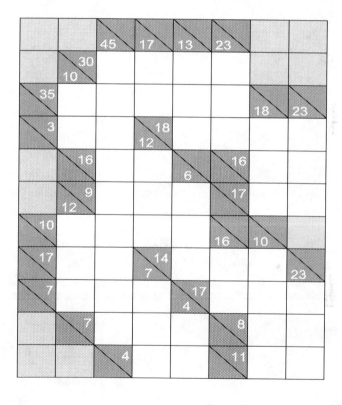

Puzzle 146

Lunch Break

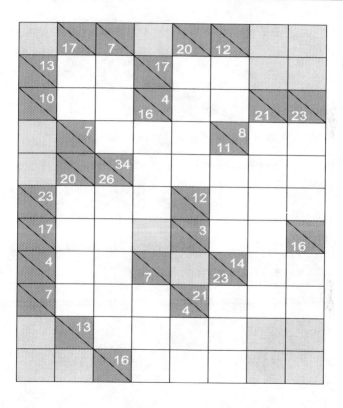

Puzzle 148

Lunch Break

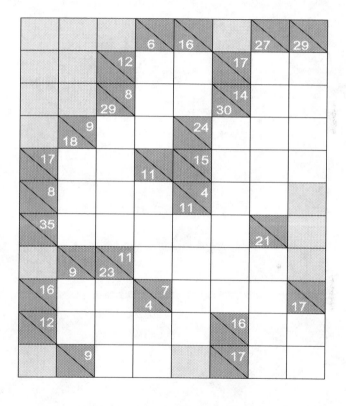

Puzzle 150

Lunch Break

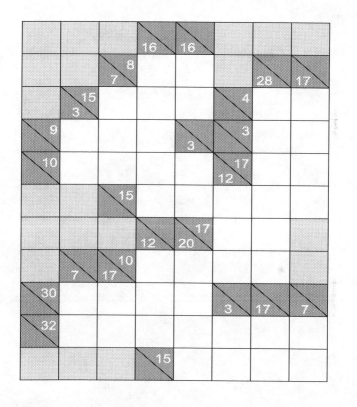

Puzzle 152

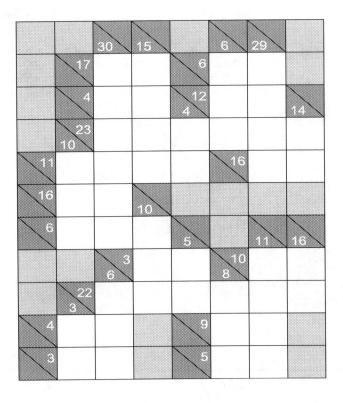

Lunch Break

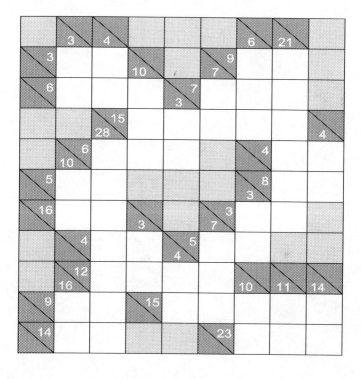

Puzzle 154

Lunch Break

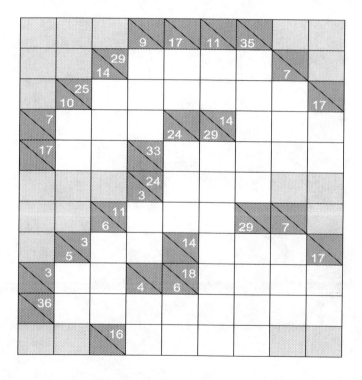

Puzzle 156

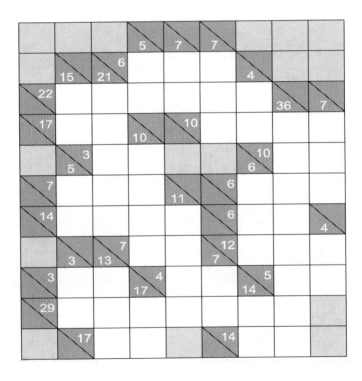

Lunch Break

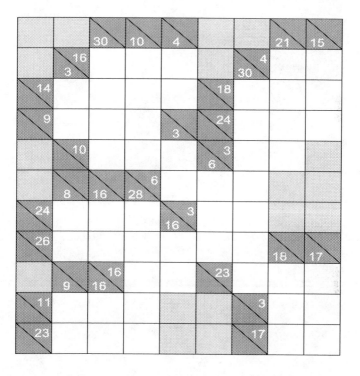

Puzzle 158

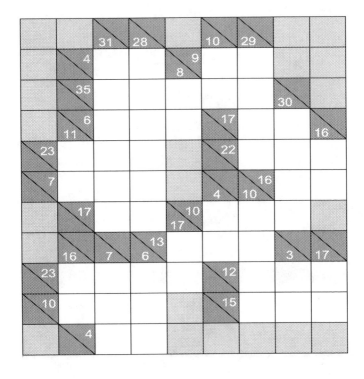

Lunch Break

Puzzle 159

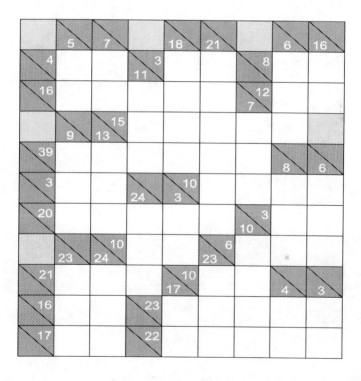

Puzzle 160

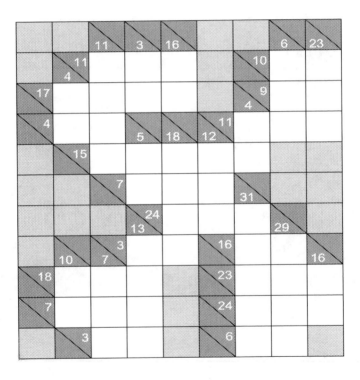

Lunch Break

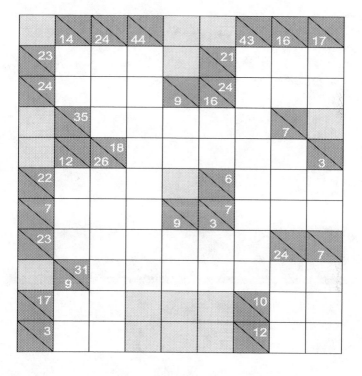

Puzzle 162

Lunch Break

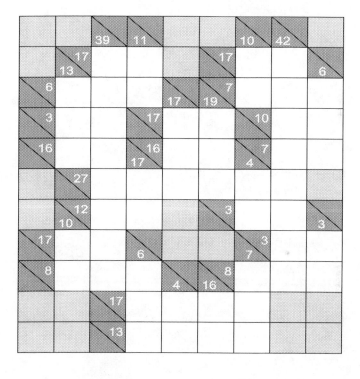

Puzzle 164

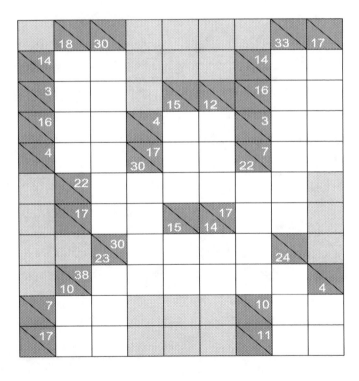

Lunch Break

Puzzle 165

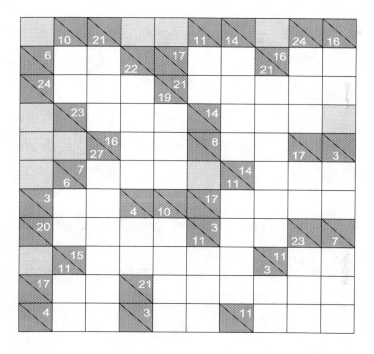

Puzzle 166

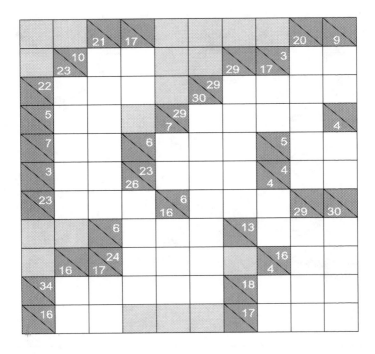

Lunch Break

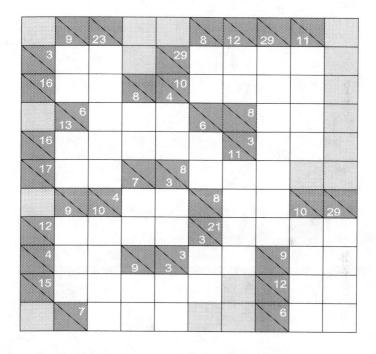

Puzzle 168

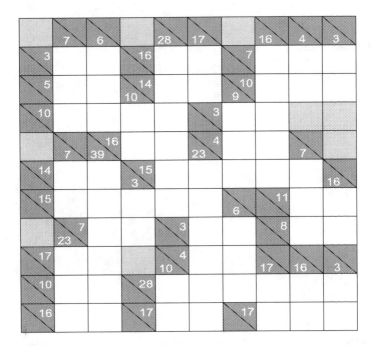

Lunch Break

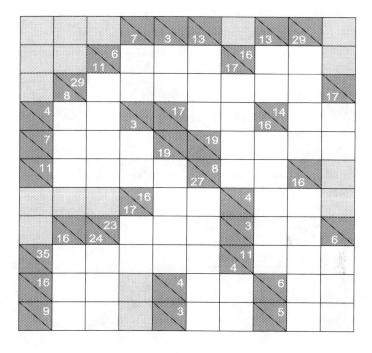

Puzzle 170

Lunch Break

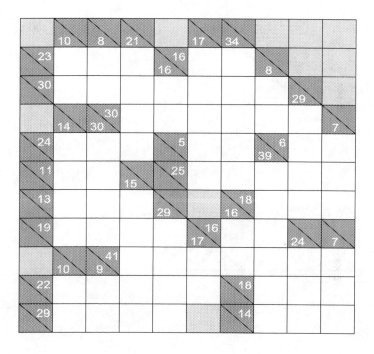

Puzzle 172

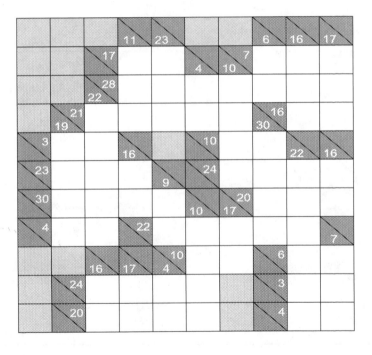

Lunch Break

Puzzle 174

Lunch Break

Puzzle 176

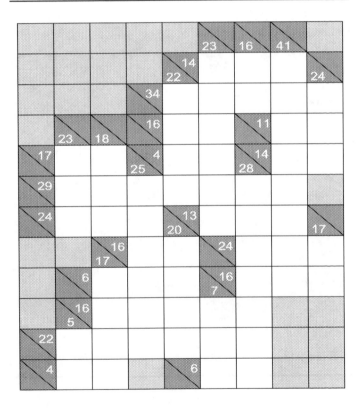

Lunch Break

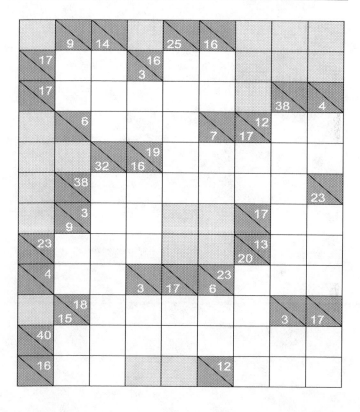

Puzzle 178

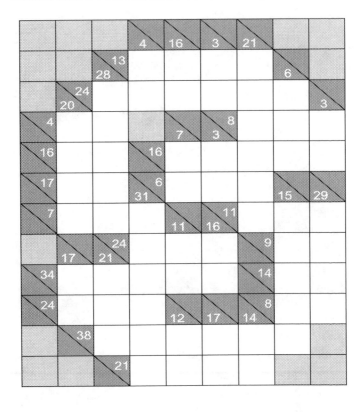

Lunch Break

Puzzle 179

Puzzle 180

Lunch Break

Summer **Kakuro**

All Nighter

Puzzles 181–201

Puzzle 181

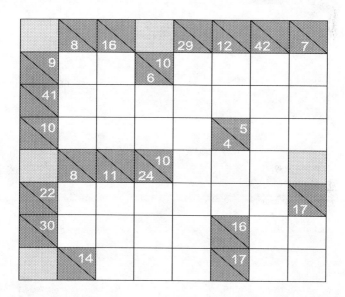

Puzzle 182

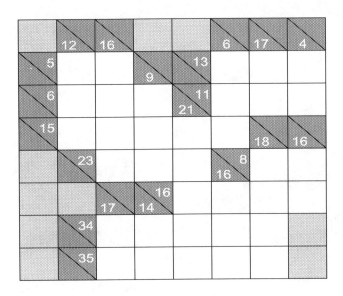

All Nighter

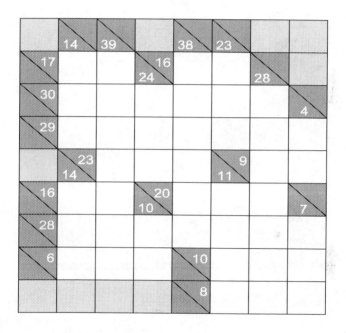

Puzzle 184

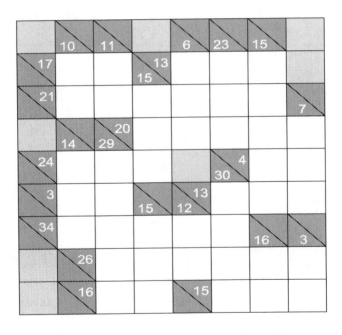

All Nighter

Puzzle 185

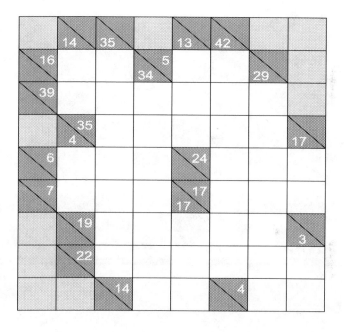

Puzzle 186

All Nighter

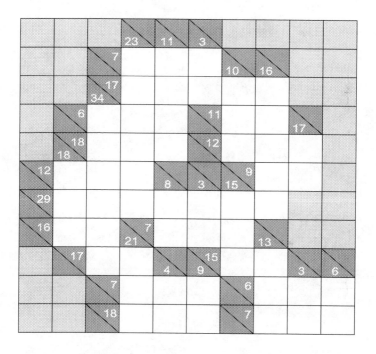

Puzzle 188

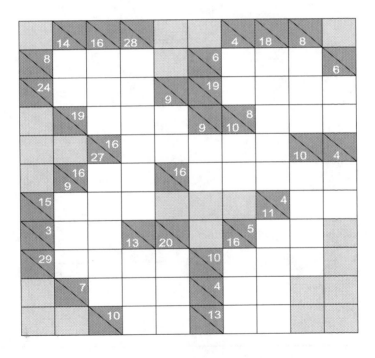

All Nighter

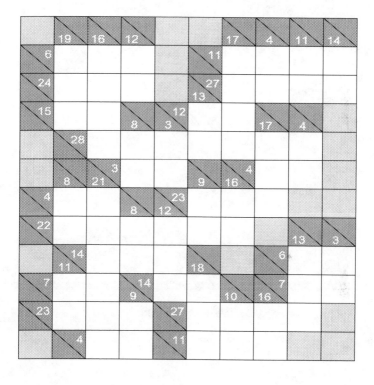

Puzzle 190

All Nighter

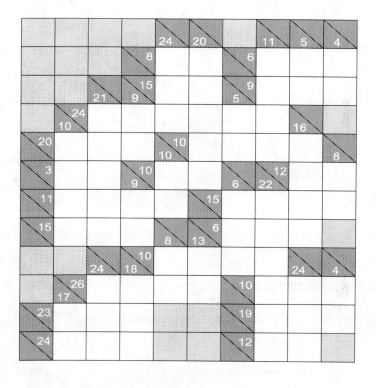

Puzzle 192

All Nighter

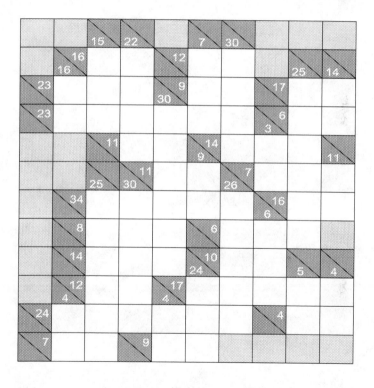

Puzzle 194

All Nighter

Puzzle 195

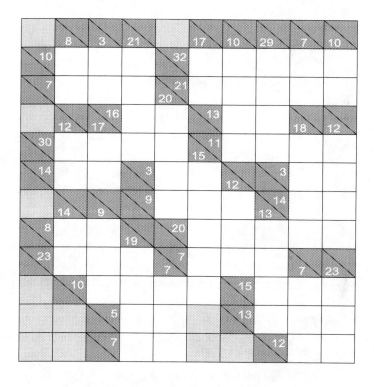

Puzzle 196

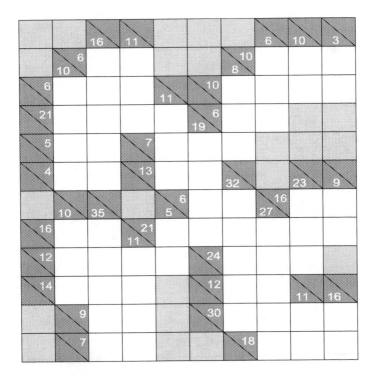

All Nighter

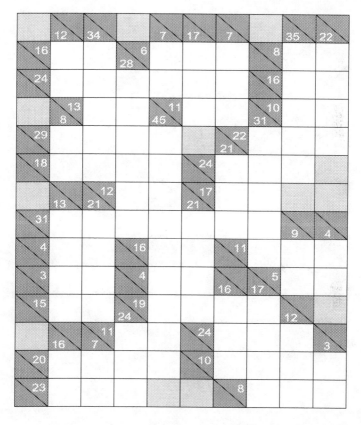

Puzzle 198

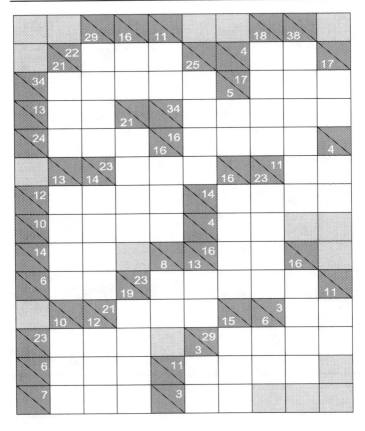

All Nighter

Puzzle 200

All Nighter

Puzzle 201

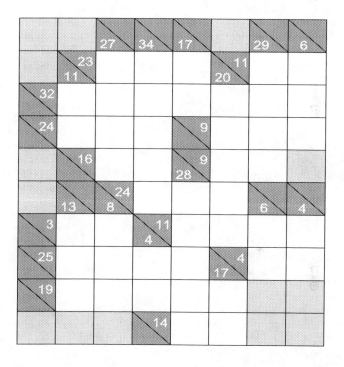

Summer **Kakuro**
Solutions

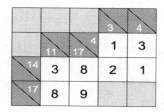

Puzzle 2

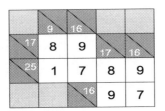

Puzzle 3

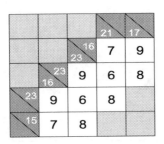

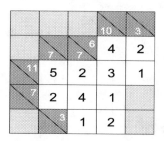

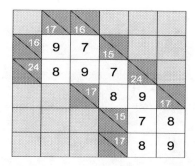

Puzzle 6

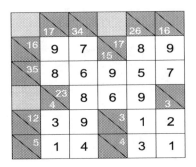

Puzzle 7

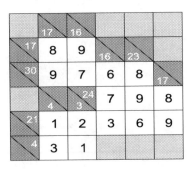

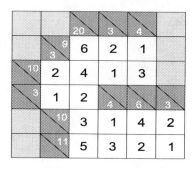

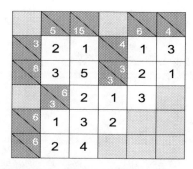

Puzzle 10

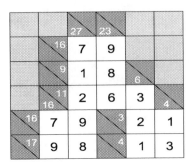

Puzzle 11

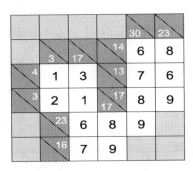

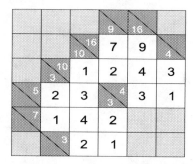

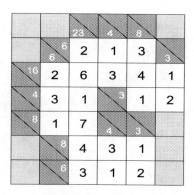

Puzzle 14

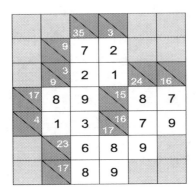

Puzzle 15

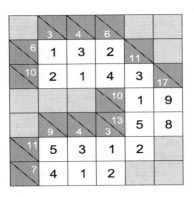

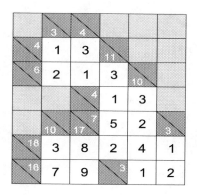

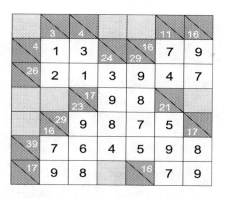

Puzzle 18

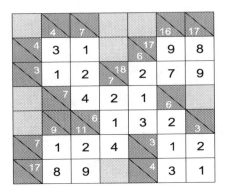

Puzzle 19

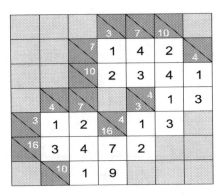

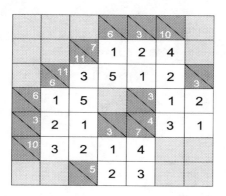

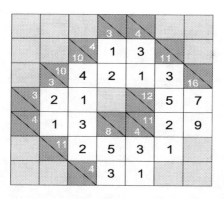

Puzzle 22

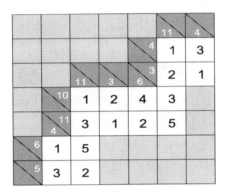

Puzzle 23

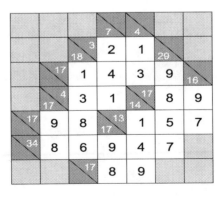

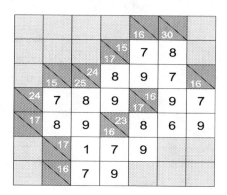

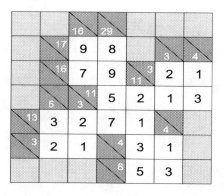

Puzzle 26

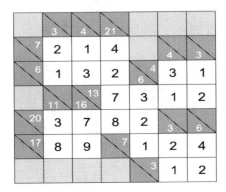

Puzzle 27

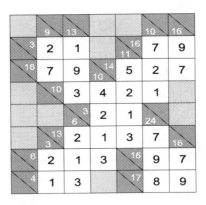

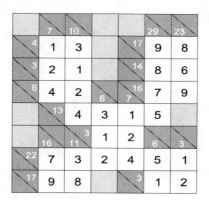

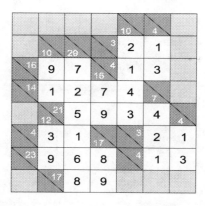

Puzzle 30

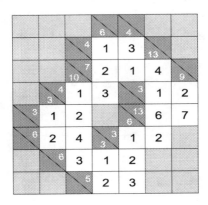

Puzzle 31

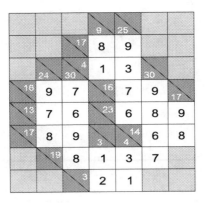

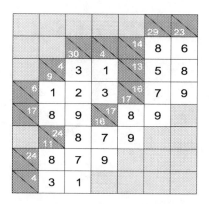

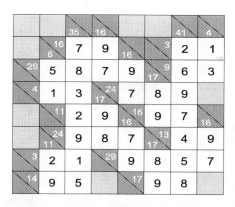

Puzzle 34

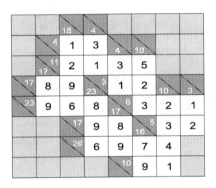

Puzzle 35

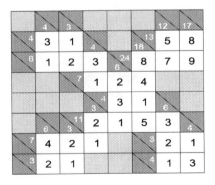

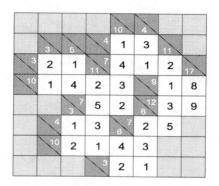

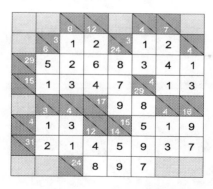

Puzzle 38

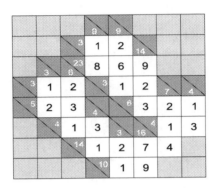

Puzzle 39

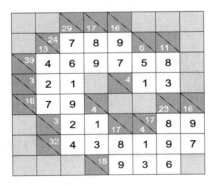

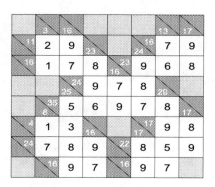

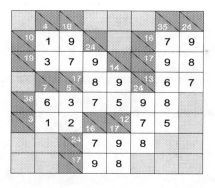

Puzzle 42

	21\	35\	17\	23\		42\	4\
\30	8	7	9	6	\4	3	1
\29	7	5	8	9	8\16	5	3
\4	1	3	24\16	8	7	9	\16
\21	5	9	7	20\24	9	4	7
17\10	1	9	7	17\16		8	9
\3	1	2	22\	9	7	6	
\17	9	8	24\	8	9	7	

Puzzle 43

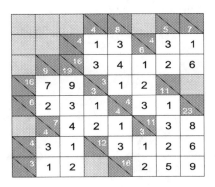

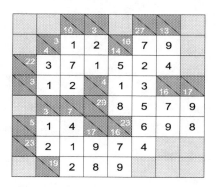

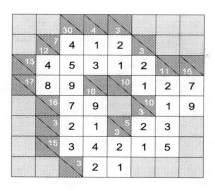

Puzzle 46

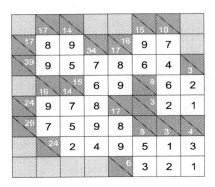

Puzzle 47

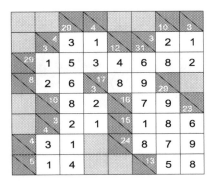

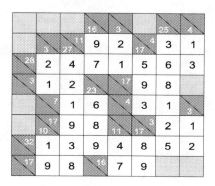

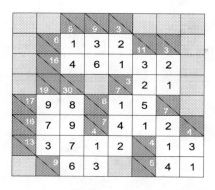

Puzzle 50

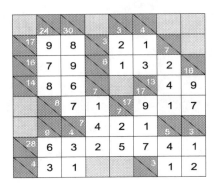

Puzzle 51

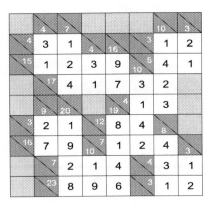

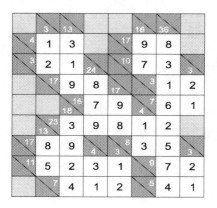

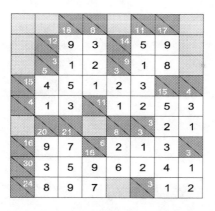

Puzzle 54

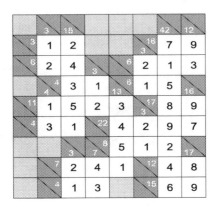

Puzzle 55

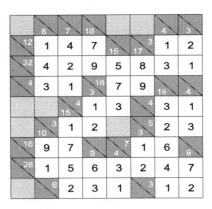

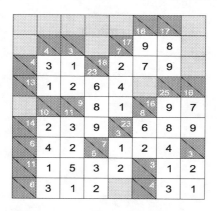

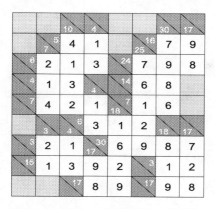

Puzzle 58

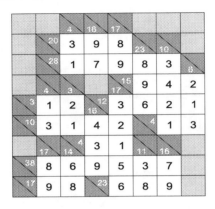

Puzzle 59

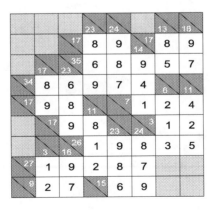

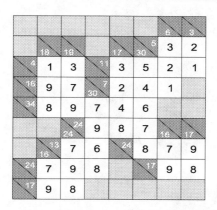

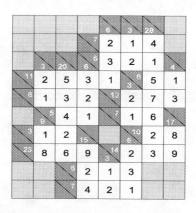

Puzzle 62

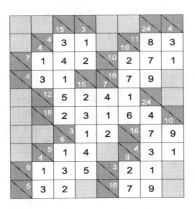

Puzzle 63

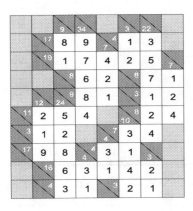

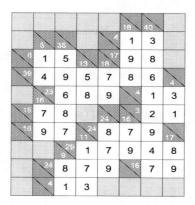

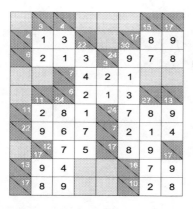

Puzzle 66

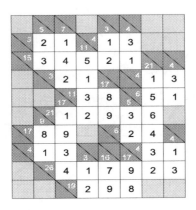

Puzzle 67

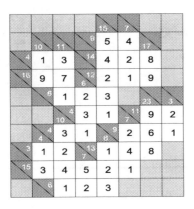

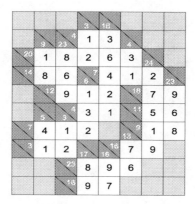

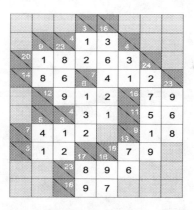

Puzzle 70

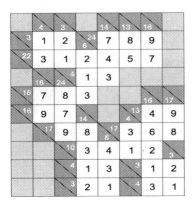

Puzzle 71

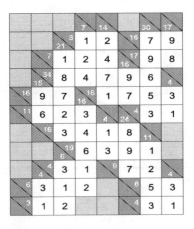

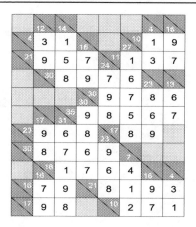

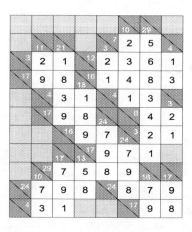

Puzzle 74

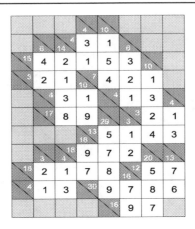

Puzzle 75

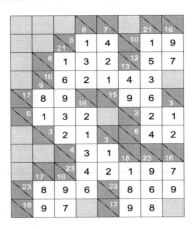

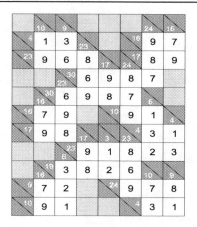

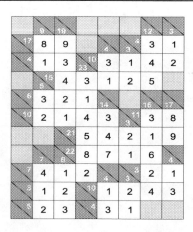

Puzzle 78

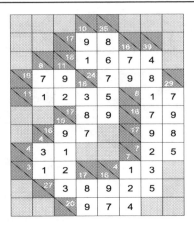

Puzzle 79

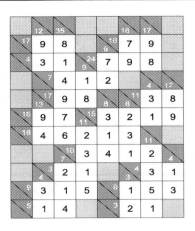

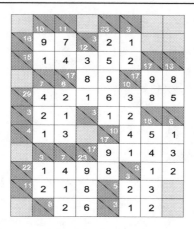

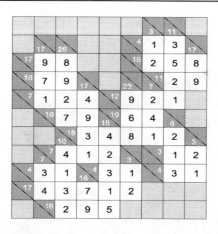

Puzzle 82

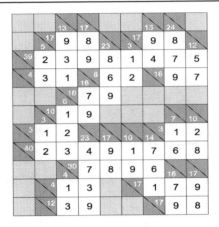

Puzzle 83

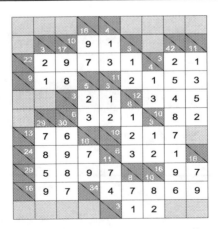

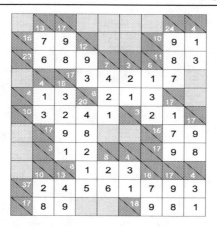

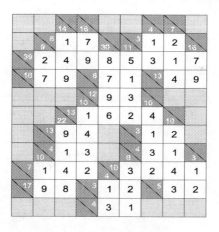

Puzzle 86

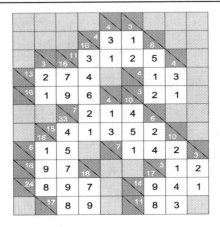

Puzzle 87

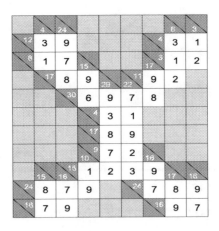

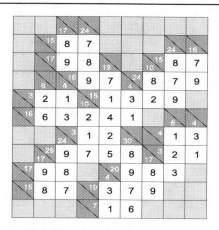

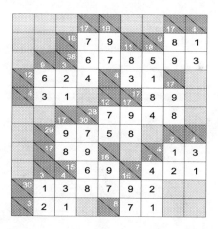

Puzzle 90

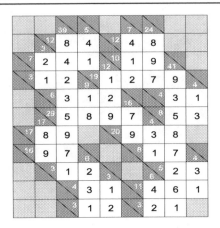

Puzzle 91

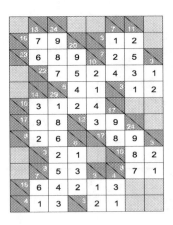

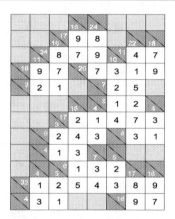

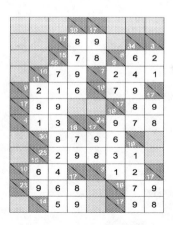

Puzzle 94

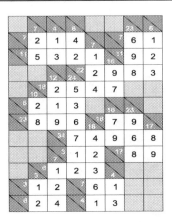

Puzzle 95

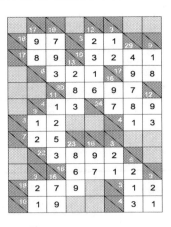

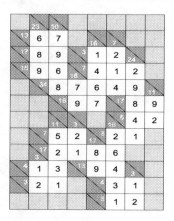

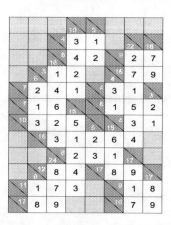

Puzzle 98

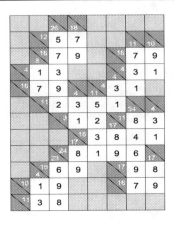

Puzzle 99

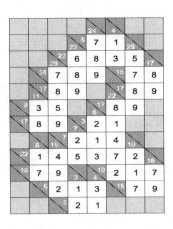

Puzzle 100

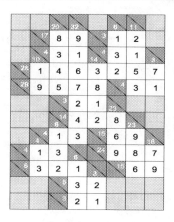

Puzzle 101

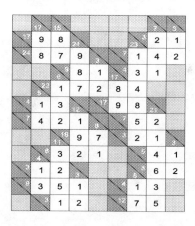

Puzzle 102

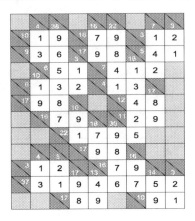

Puzzle 103

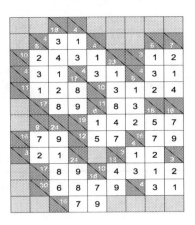

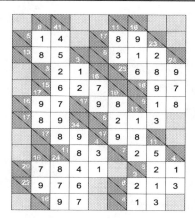

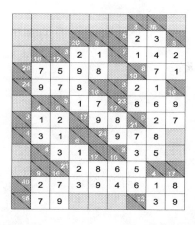

Puzzle 106

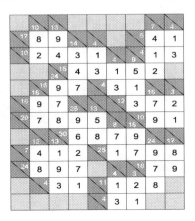

Puzzle 107

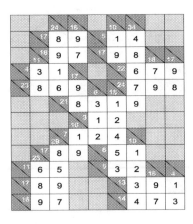

Puzzle 108

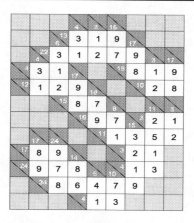

Puzzle 109

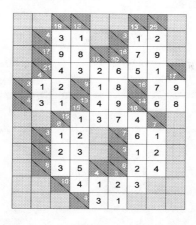

Puzzle 110

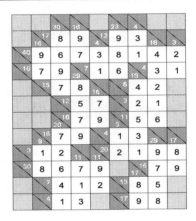

Puzzle 111

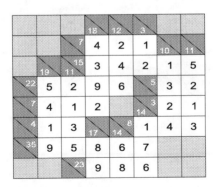

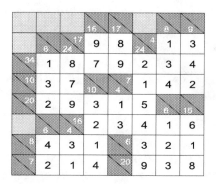

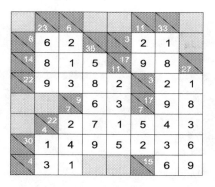

Puzzle 114

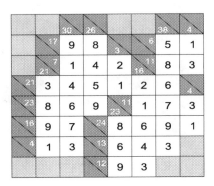

Puzzle 115

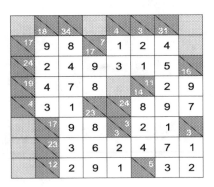

Puzzle 116

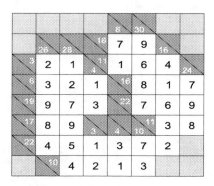

Puzzle 117

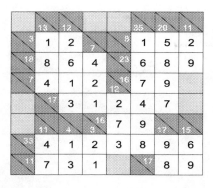

Puzzle 118

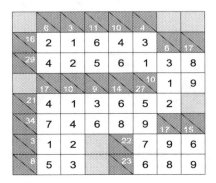

Puzzle 119

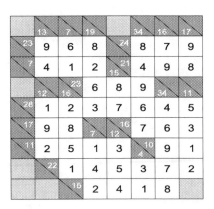

Puzzle 120

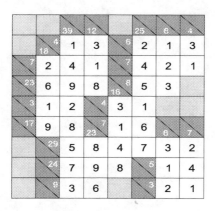

Puzzle 121

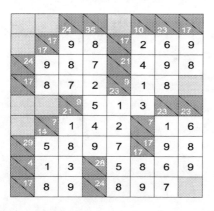

Puzzle 122

	12\	16\		25\	24\	17\	
16\	9	7	23\\21	8	6	9	
38\	3	9	5	6	7	8	
		6\	1	2	3		
	15\	23\\21	6	9	8		
6\	1	3	2	3\	6\	24\	
25\	4	1	7	2	3	8	17\
10\	2	8	19\	1	2	7	9
17\	8	9		18\	1	9	8

Puzzle 123

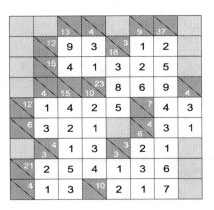

		13\	4\		9\	37\	
	12\	9	3	3\\16	1	2	
	16\	4	1	3	2	5	
	4\	15\	23\\10	8	6	9	4\
12\	1	4	2	5	7\	4	3
6\	3	2	1		4\\6	3	1
	3\\4	1	3	3\\3	2	1	
21\	2	5	4	1	3	6	
4\	1	3	10\	2	1	7	

Puzzle 124

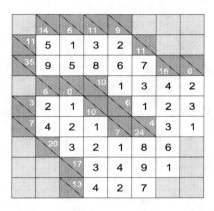

Puzzle 125

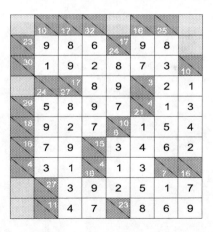

Puzzle 126

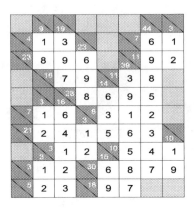

Puzzle 127

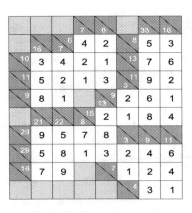

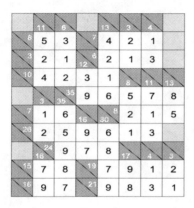

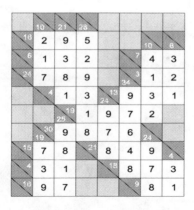

Puzzle 130

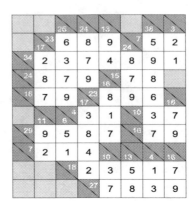

Puzzle 131

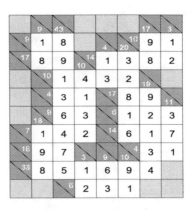

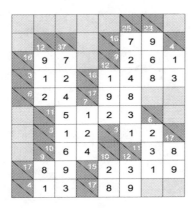

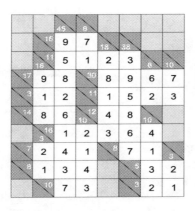

Puzzle 134

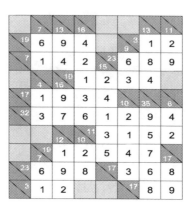

Puzzle 135

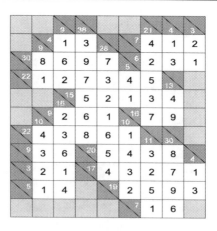

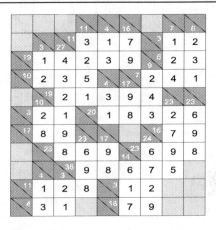

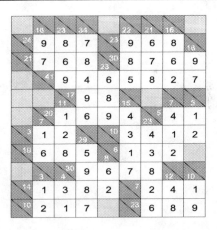

Puzzle 138

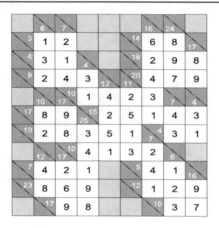

Puzzle 139

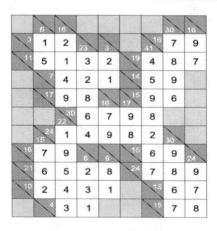

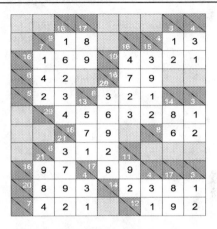

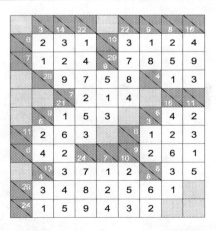

Puzzle 142

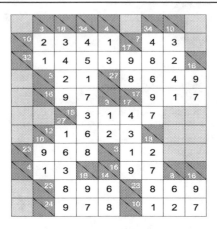

Puzzle 143

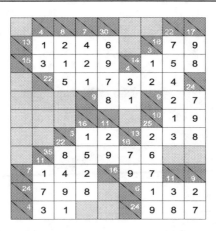

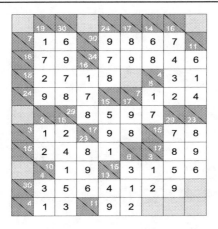

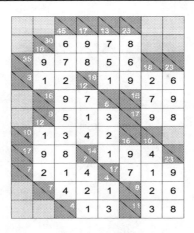

Puzzle 146

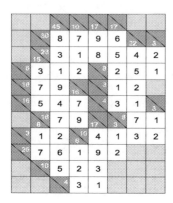

Puzzle 147

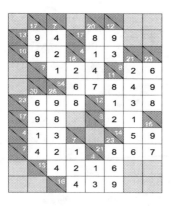

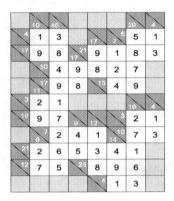

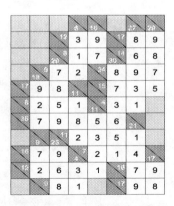

Puzzle 150

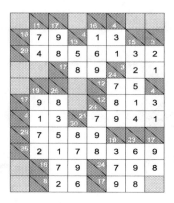

Puzzle 151

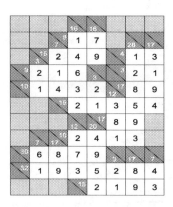

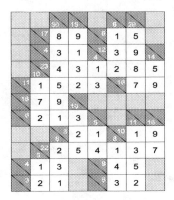

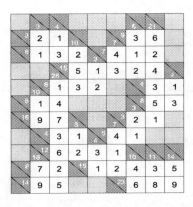

Puzzle 154

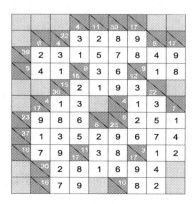

Puzzle 155

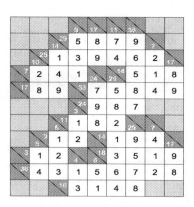

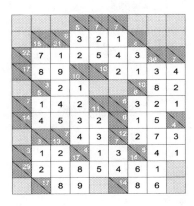

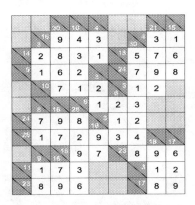

Puzzle 158

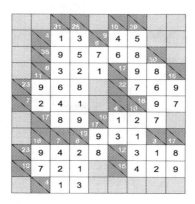

Puzzle 159

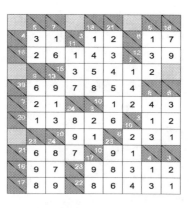

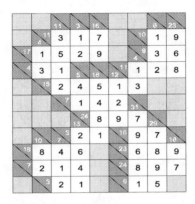

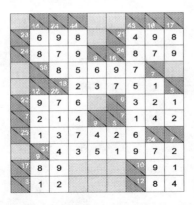

Puzzle 162

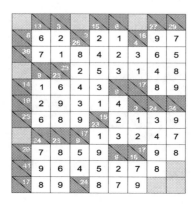

Puzzle 163

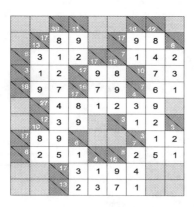

Puzzle 164

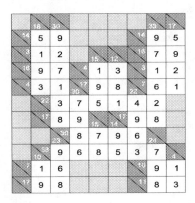

Puzzle 165

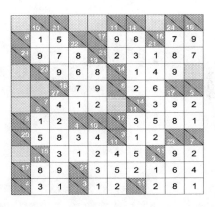

Puzzle 166

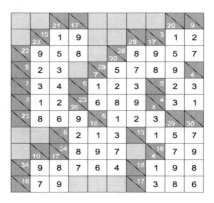

Puzzle 167

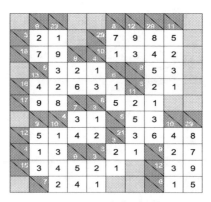

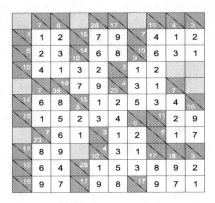

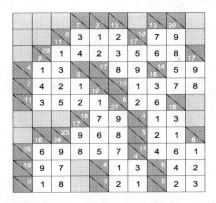

Puzzle 170

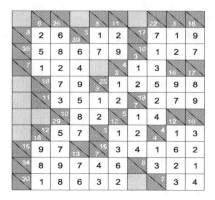

Puzzle 171

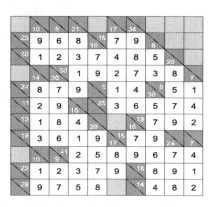

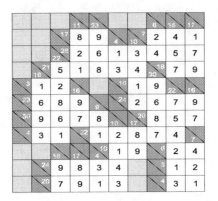

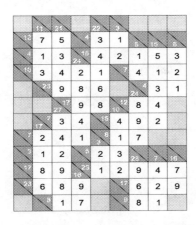

Puzzle 174

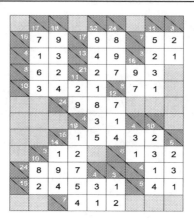

Puzzle 175

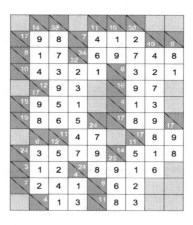

Puzzle 176

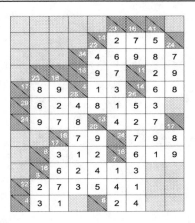

Puzzle 177

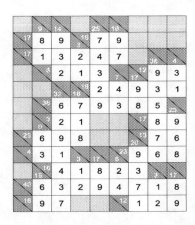

Puzzle 178

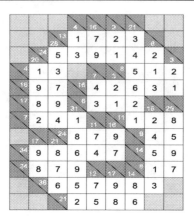

Puzzle 179

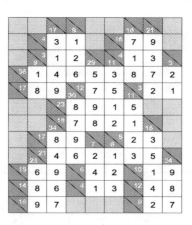

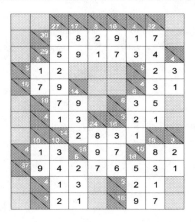

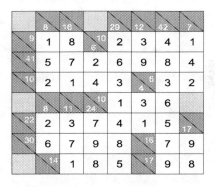

Puzzle 182

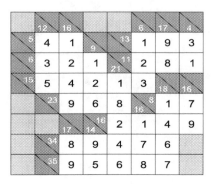

Puzzle 183

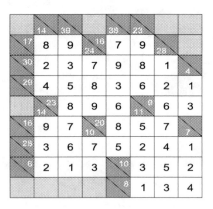

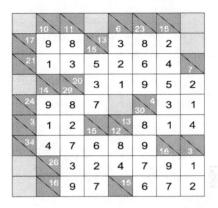

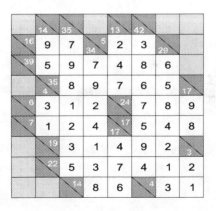

Puzzle 186

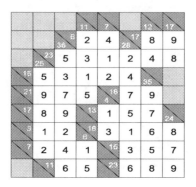

Puzzle 187

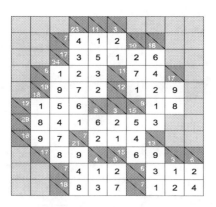

Puzzle 188

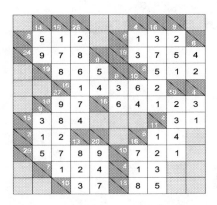

Puzzle 189

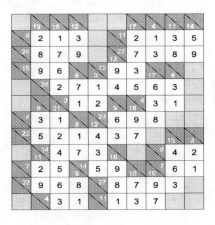

Puzzle 190

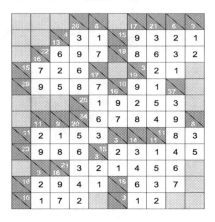

Puzzle 191

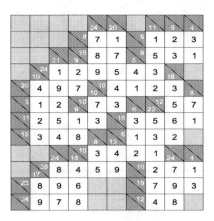

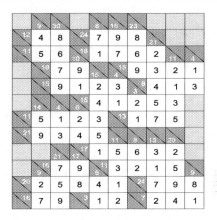

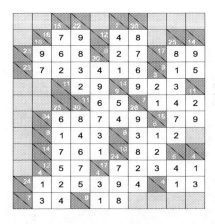

Puzzle 194

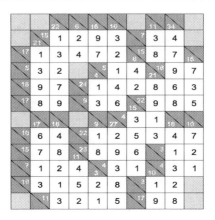

Puzzle 195

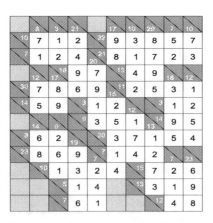

Puzzle 196

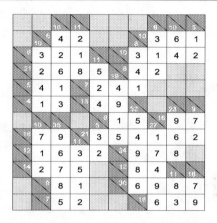

Puzzle 197

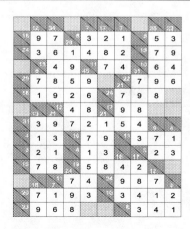

Puzzle 198

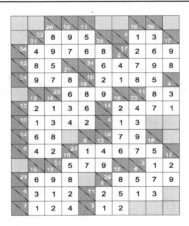

Puzzle 199

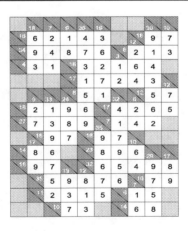

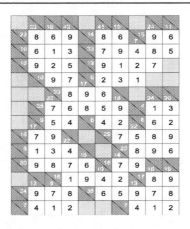

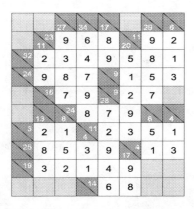

Summer **Kakuro**
Cheat Sheets

2-digit combinations

$3 = 1+2$

$4 = 1+3$

$5 = 1+4, 2+3$

$6 = 1+5, 2+4$

$7 = 1+6, 2+5, 3+4$

$8 = 1+7, 2+6, 3+5$

$9 = 1+8, 2+7, 3+6, 4+5$

$10 = 1+9, 2+8, 3+7, 4+6$

$11 = 2+9, 3+8, 4+7, 5+6$

$12 = 3+9, 4+8, 5+7$

$13 = 4+9, 5+8, 6+7$

$14 = 5+9, 6+8$

$15 = 6+9, 7+8$

$16 = 7+9$

$17 = 8+9$

3-digit combinations

$6 = 1+2+3$

$7 = 1+2+4$

$8 = 1+2+5, 1+3+4$

$9 = 1+2+6, 1+3+5, 2+3+4$

$10 = 1+2+7, 1+3+6, 1+4+5, 2+3+5$

$11 = 1+2+8, 1+3+7, 1+4+6, 2+3+6, 2+4+5$

$12 = 1+2+9, 1+3+8, 1+4+7, 1+5+6, 2+3+7, 2+4+6, 3+4+5$

$13 = 1+3+9, 1+4+8, 1+5+7, 2+3+8, 2+4+7, 2+5+6, 3+4+6$

$14 = 1+4+9, 1+5+8, 1+6+7, 2+3+9, 2+4+8, 2+5+7, 3+4+7, 3+5+6$

$15 = 1+5+9, 1+6+8, 2+4+9, 2+5+8, 2+6+7, 3+4+8, 3+5+7, 4+5+6$

$16 = 1+6+9, 1+7+8, 2+5+9, 2+6+8, 3+4+9, 3+5+8, 3+6+7, 4+5+7$

$17 = 1+7+9, 2+6+9, 2+7+8, 3+5+9, 3+6+8, 4+5+8, 4+6+7$

$18 = 1+8+9, 2+7+9, 3+6+9, 3+7+8, 4+5+9, 4+6+8, 5+6+7$

$19 = 2+8+9, 3+7+9, 4+6+9, 4+7+8, 5+6+8$

$20 = 3+8+9, 4+7+9, 5+6+9, 5+7+8$

$21 = 4+8+9, 5+7+9, 6+7+8$

22 = 5+8+9, 6+7+9

23 = 6+8+9

24 = 7+8+9

4-digit combinations

10 = 1+2+3+4

11 = 1+2+3+5

12 = 1+2+3+6, 1+2+4+5

13 = 1+2+3+7, 1+2+4+6,
1+3+4+5

14 = 1+2+3+8, 1+2+4+7,
1+2+5+6, 1+3+4+6,
2+3+4+5

15 = 1+2+3+9, 1+2+4+8,
1+2+5+7, 1+3+4+7,
1+3+5+6, 2+3+4+6

16 = 1+2+4+9, 1+2+5+8,
1+2+6+7, 1+3+4+8,
1+3+5+7, 1+4+5+6,
2+3+4+7, 2+3+5+6

17 = 1+2+5+9, 1+2+6+8,
1+3+4+9, 1+3+5+8,
1+3+6+7, 1+4+5+7,
2+3+4+8, 2+3+5+7,
2+4+5+6

18 = 1+2+6+9, 1+2+7+8,
1+3+5+9, 1+3+6+8,
1+4+5+8, 1+4+6+7,
2+3+4+9, 2+3+5+8,
2+3+6+7, 2+4+5+7,
3+4+5+6

19 = 1+2+7+9, 1+3+6+9,
1+3+7+8, 1+4+5+9,
1+4+6+8, 1+5+6+7,
2+3+5+9, 2+3+6+8,
2+4+5+8, 2+4+6+7,
3+4+5+7

20 = 1+2+8+9, 1+3+7+9,
1+4+6+9, 1+4+7+8,
1+5+6+8, 2+3+6+9,
2+3+7+8, 2+4+5+9,
2+4+6+8, 2+5+6+7,
3+4+5+8, 3+4+6+7

21 = 1+3+8+9, 1+4+7+9,
1+5+6+9, 1+5+7+8,
2+3+7+9, 2+4+6+9,
2+4+7+8, 2+5+6+8,
3+4+5+9, 3+4+6+8,
3+5+6+7

22 = 1+4+8+9, 1+5+7+9,
1+6+7+8, 2+3+8+9,
2+4+7+9, 2+5+6+9,
2+5+7+8, 3+4+6+9,
3+4+7+8, 3+5+6+8,
4+5+6+7

23 = 1+5+8+9, 1+6+7+9,
2+4+8+9, 2+5+7+9,
2+6+7+8, 3+4+7+9,
3+5+6+9, 3+5+7+8,
4+5+6+8

24 = 1+6+8+9, 2+5+8+9,
2+6+7+9, 3+4+8+9,
3+5+7+9, 3+6+7+8,
4+5+6+9, 4+5+7+8

25 = 1+7+8+9, 2+6+8+9,
3+5+8+9, 3+6+7+9,
4+5+7+9, 4+6+7+8

26 = 2+7+8+9, 3+6+8+9,
4+5+8+9, 4+6+7+9,
5+6+7+8

27 = 3+7+8+9, 4+6+8+9,
5+6+7+9

28 = 4+7+8+9, 5+6+8+9

29 = 5+7+8+9

30 = 6+7+8+9

5-digit combinations

15 = 1+2+3+4+5

16 = 1+2+3+4+6

17 = 1+2+3+4+7, 1+2+3+5+6

18 = 1+2+3+4+8, 1+2+3+5+7,
1+2+4+5+6

19 = 1+2+3+4+9, 1+2+3+5+8,
1+2+3+6+7, 1+2+4+5+7,
1+3+4+5+6

20 = 1+2+3+5+9, 1+2+3+6+8,
1+2+4+5+8, 1+2+4+6+7,
1+3+4+5+7, 2+3+4+5+6

21 = 1+2+3+6+9, 1+2+3+7+8,
1+2+4+5+9, 1+2+4+6+8,
1+2+5+6+7, 1+3+4+5+8,
1+3+4+6+7, 2+3+4+5+7

22 = 1+2+3+7+9, 1+2+4+6+9,
1+2+4+7+8, 1+2+5+6+8,
1+3+4+5+9, 1+3+4+6+8,
1+3+5+6+7, 2+3+4+5+8,
2+3+4+6+7

23 = 1+2+3+8+9, 1+2+4+7+9,
1+2+5+6+9, 1+2+5+7+8,
1+3+4+6+9, 1+3+4+7+8,
1+3+5+6+8, 1+4+5+6+7,
2+3+4+5+9, 2+3+4+6+8,
2+3+5+6+7

24 = 1+2+4+8+9, 1+2+5+7+9,
1+2+6+7+8, 1+3+4+7+9,
1+3+5+6+9, 1+3+5+7+8,
1+4+5+6+8, 2+3+4+6+9,
2+3+4+7+8, 2+3+5+6+8,
2+4+5+6+7

25 = 1+2+5+8+9, 1+2+6+7+9,
1+3+4+8+9, 1+3+5+7+9,
1+3+6+7+8, 1+4+5+6+9,
1+4+5+7+8, 2+3+4+7+9,
2+3+5+6+9, 2+3+5+7+8,
2+4+5+6+8, 3+4+5+6+7

26 = 1+2+6+8+9, 1+3+5+8+9,
1+3+6+7+9, 1+4+5+7+9,
1+4+6+7+8, 2+3+4+8+9,
2+3+5+7+9, 2+3+6+7+8,
2+4+5+6+9, 2+4+5+7+8,
3+4+5+6+8

27 = 1+2+7+8+9, 1+3+6+8+9,
1+4+5+8+9, 1+4+6+7+9,
1+5+6+7+8, 2+3+5+8+9,
2+3+6+7+9, 2+4+5+7+9,
2+4+6+7+8, 3+4+5+6+9,
3+4+5+7+8

28 = 1+3+7+8+9, 1+4+6+8+9,
1+5+6+7+9, 2+3+6+8+9,
2+4+5+8+9, 2+4+6+7+9,
2+5+6+7+8, 3+4+5+7+9,
3+4+6+7+8

29 = 1+4+7+8+9, 1+5+6+8+9,
2+3+7+8+9, 2+4+6+8+9,
2+5+6+7+9, 3+4+5+8+9,
3+4+6+7+9, 3+5+6+7+8

30 = 1+5+7+8+9, 2+4+7+8+9,
2+5+6+8+9, 3+4+6+8+9,
3+5+6+7+9, 4+5+6+7+8

31 = 1+6+7+8+9, 2+5+7+8+9,
3+4+7+8+9, 3+5+6+8+9,
4+5+6+7+9

32 = 2+6+7+8+9, 3+5+7+8+9,
4+5+6+8+9

33 = 3+6+7+8+9, 4+5+7+8+9

34 = 4+6+7+8+9

35 = 5+6+7+8+9

6-digit combinations

21 = 1+2+3+4+5+6

22 = 1+2+3+4+5+7

23 = 1+2+3+4+5+8,
     1+2+3+4+6+7

24 = 1+2+3+4+5+9,
     1+2+3+4+6+8,
     1+2+3+5+6+7

25 = 1+2+3+4+6+9,
     1+2+3+4+7+8,
     1+2+3+5+6+8,
     1+2+4+5+6+7

26 = 1+2+3+4+7+9,
     1+2+3+5+6+9,
     1+2+3+5+7+8,
     1+2+4+5+6+8,
     1+3+4+5+6+7

27 = 1+2+3+4+8+9,
     1+2+3+5+7+9,
     1+2+3+6+7+8,
     1+2+4+5+6+9,
     1+2+4+5+7+8,
     1+3+4+5+6+8,
     2+3+4+5+6+7

28 = 1+2+3+5+8+9,
     1+2+3+6+7+9,
     1+2+4+5+7+9,
     1+2+4+6+7+8,
     1+3+4+5+6+9,
     1+3+4+5+7+8,
     2+3+4+5+6+8

29 = 1+2+3+6+8+9,
     1+2+4+5+8+9,
     1+2+4+6+7+9,
     1+2+5+6+7+8,
     1+3+4+5+7+9,
     1+3+4+6+7+8,

2+3+4+5+6+9,
2+3+4+5+7+8

30 = 1+2+3+7+8+9,
     1+2+4+6+8+9,
     1+2+5+6+7+9,
     1+3+4+5+8+9,
     1+3+4+6+7+9,
     1+3+5+6+7+8,
     2+3+4+5+7+9,
     2+3+4+6+7+8

31 = 1+2+4+7+8+9,
     1+2+5+6+8+9,
     1+3+4+6+8+9,
     1+3+5+6+7+9,
     1+4+5+6+7+8,
     2+3+4+5+8+9,
     2+3+4+6+7+9,
     2+3+5+6+7+8

32 = 1+2+5+7+8+9,
     1+3+4+7+8+9,
     1+3+5+6+8+9,
     1+4+5+6+7+9,
     2+3+4+6+8+9,
     2+3+5+6+7+9,
     2+4+5+6+7+8

33 = 1+2+6+7+8+9,
     1+3+5+7+8+9,
     1+4+5+6+8+9,
     2+3+4+7+8+9,
     2+3+5+6+8+9,
     2+4+5+6+7+9,
     3+4+5+6+7+8

34 = 1+3+6+7+8+9,
     1+4+5+7+8+9,
     2+3+5+7+8+9,
     2+4+5+6+8+9,
     3+4+5+6+7+9

$35 = 1+4+6+7+8+9,$
$ 2+3+6+7+8+9,$
$ 2+4+5+7+8+9,$
$ 3+4+5+6+8+9$

$36 = 1+5+6+7+8+9,$
$ 2+4+6+7+8+9,$
$ 3+4+5+7+8+9$

$37 = 2+5+6+7+8+9,$
$ 3+4+6+7+8+9$

$38 = 3+5+6+7+8+9$

$39 = 4+5+6+7+8+9$

7-digit combinations

$28 = 1+2+3+4+5+6+7$

$29 = 1+2+3+4+5+6+8$

$30 = 1+2+3+4+5+6+9,$
$ 1+2+3+4+5+7+8$

$31 = 1+2+3+4+5+7+9,$
$ 1+2+3+4+6+7+8$

$32 = 1+2+3+4+5+8+9,$
$ 1+2+3+4+6+7+9,$
$ 1+2+3+5+6+7+8$

$33 = 1+2+3+4+6+8+9,$
$ 1+2+3+5+6+7+9,$
$ 1+2+4+5+6+7+8$

$34 = 1+2+3+4+7+8+9,$
$ 1+2+3+5+6+8+9,$
$ 1+2+4+5+6+7+9,$
$ 1+3+4+5+6+7+8$

$35 = 1+2+3+5+7+8+9,$
$ 1+2+4+5+6+8+9,$
$ 1+3+4+5+6+7+9,$
$ 2+3+4+5+6+7+8$

$36 = 1+2+3+6+7+8+9,$
$ 1+2+4+5+7+8+9,$
$ 1+3+4+5+6+8+9,$
$ 2+3+4+5+6+7+9$

$37 = 1+2+4+6+7+8+9,$
$ 1+3+4+5+7+8+9,$
$ 2+3+4+5+6+8+9$

$38 = 1+2+5+6+7+8+9,$
$ 1+3+4+6+7+8+9,$
$ 2+3+4+5+7+8+9$

$39 = 1+3+5+6+7+8+9,$
$ 2+3+4+6+7+8+9$

$40 = 1+4+5+6+7+8+9,$
$ 2+3+5+6+7+8+9$

$41 = 2+4+5+6+7+8+9$

$42 = 3+4+5+6+7+8+9$

8-digit combinations

$36 = 1+2+3+4+5+6+7+8$

$37 = 1+2+3+4+5+6+7+9$

$38 = 1+2+3+4+5+6+8+9$

$39 = 1+2+3+4+5+7+8+9$

$40 = 1+2+3+4+6+7+8+9$

$41 = 1+2+3+5+6+7+8+9$

$42 = 1+2+4+5+6+7+8+9$

$43 = 1+3+4+5+6+7+8+9$

$44 = 2+3+4+5+6+7+8+9$

9-digit combination

$45 = 1+2+3+4+5+6+7+8+9$

Printed in the United States
By Bookmasters